How to Buy a House
Without Killing Anyone

Andrew Boast FMAAT

CONTENTS

ACKNOWLEDGMENTS

I cannot thank my editors enough. I've worked with them for years and I learn so much from their technical knowledge and client focused approach. I appreciate their input and their patience.

Having two highly experienced solicitors editing this book means my insider guidance is backed with their technical expertise.

Sarah Haller, Property Solicitor

Sarah is a Partner at Chadwick Lawrence Solicitors in West Yorkshire. She is Head of Conveyancing at her practice, in addition to being the firm's Money Laundering Reporting Officer and Senior Responsible Officer for the Law Society's Conveyancing Quality Scheme.

Sarah's whole career in the legal profession has been at Chadwick Lawrence where she started as a temporary legal secretary 25 years ago. She was appointed as a trainee solicitor in 1999, qualified as a solicitor in 2000, became an Associate in 2008 and was promoted to Partner in 2009. In 2014 she completed a Master's in Business Administration.

For most of her time at the firm she worked on client files but now, with a department of almost 80 people to keep in check (alongside her senior management team), she sticks to management, compliance, procedure, strategy, and external conveyancing relationships.

Luciana Ispani, Conveyancing Solicitor

Lucy qualified as a Solicitor in September 1997, and has since then worked in property. She started her career with residential property sales and purchases, and then took on plot sales for a large, well-known developer. She progressed to land acquisition and set up, for the same developer, and another, smaller, regional developer.

From there she moved to a small, niche, City of London firm and undertook mainly commercial property work, with some residential work. Since then, she has worked in a few different firms carrying out a mixed role of both residential and commercial property work, with some development along the way.

She estimates to have helped over 10,000 people, over the years, and is most grateful for the wonderful experience she has had, especially being able to practice with a mixed caseload, the lovely people she has worked with, and those that have mentored her along the way.

Caragh Bailey, Content Guru

Thanks also to my editor and proof-reader. Caragh is my senior copy writer of online content. She joined my company a few years ago, bringing her natural talent for writing. She has contributed excellent articles and editorial pieces to my websites and specialises in Search Engine Optimisation and Strategy.

She has a keen eye for structure, grammar, and flow, and I appreciate all her help. Proof is in the pudding and this pudding would be a mess without Caragh's attention to detail.

INTRODUCTION

...Why should I bother reading this book?

Simple, this book could be the difference between every mover's dream: buying and moving into your new home stress free; or stress, missed deadlines, legal disasters, building defects, and possibly the collapse of the whole transaction. (Costing you a small fortune, a head full of grey hairs, and driving you to threaten the life of your solicitor, lender, co-owners, parents, partner, or some combination of all five).

Think I'm being dramatic? After more than 22 years working in the conveyancing sector, I've seen for myself how a transaction can fall apart, through a lack of understanding, poor communication, and anger, as pride kicks in and you get fed up waiting. This can be avoided if you know the process, have good communication on progress, and set out with an awareness of common obstacles and how to overcome them.

I searched high and low for this type of guide and all I found were volumes of textbooks that I'm sure make sense to a lawyer but are useless to a first-time buyer. They also lack any real-life insider tips and advice to work out the best way forward. Solicitors lean away from stuff like this – they prefer to explain the risk and leave it to you to decide your next steps.

This is why I wrote this book, and this is why you need to read it. I cover every stage of the conveyancing process, from how to save up to buy a house, making an offer, through each stage of the purchase, to what you do after you move in. It has tips on ways to save money and cut time, it'll guide you on what timeframes to expect and although I say, "How to buy a house", it covers flats and maisonettes as well.

You can jump to different parts of the book as you progress through buying and if you hit a hurdle come back and read the chapter related to that stage as it'll explain what you can do.

You'll probably think, as you read this *'Why didn't they teach us this at school?!'* and *'If only auntie Jenny knew this when she sold her flat to buy with her bloke'*. On average, in England and Wales, you buy a new home 4 to 5 times in your life. So, it's understandable that friends and family can't always remember the process and pass their wisdom on. What they probably do remember are the frustrations and stress of having to wait, and wondering what is going on.

Anyway, why do I need to know what's going on? that's what I pay a solicitor for? Right? Wrong. So wrong. Understanding what is going on during the process allows you to make informed decisions as to how to proceed, as well as realise that sending 20 emails a day chasing your solicitor isn't going to make them move any quicker. There are things beyond your (and even your solicitor's) control, I'll explain these as I go along.

Two of the biggest complaints made about the conveyancing process are:

1. I can't get hold of my solicitor; and
2. I don't know what's going on.

For most first-time buyers the conveyancing process is a mystery and feels like a torture of waiting and not knowing. I mean you have the money, the seller has the property, why can't you just sign a contract, pay the money, and get the keys? Because, you may be buying a property that has an issue which means you can't sell it for the price you paid. There are plenty of issues that can cause this, subsidence, cladding, major works, sellers who've undertaken works without appropriate sign off at the council, or breaches to your obligations in your title.

A house is the most expensive thing you'll ever buy, so doing proper due diligence isn't a pain, it is a necessity; to avoid wasting your money or finding yourself trying to sue your solicitor for bad advice.

This book bridges the gap between you and your solicitor, with real life tips and guidance on strategy and tactics that I have used to help my clients since I started working in this sector in 2000. Often solicitors forget that for homebuyers, it's not just about the law. There is so much technicality and strategy in the buying process that feelings and emotions often get overlooked.

What you rarely get told about when buying a home is the psychology of the transaction; how transactions completely fall apart because of a misunderstanding or because the pride of one of the parties has been dented. I've seen how these types of transactions can be rescued using tried and tested practices to bring both sides back to the table and reach the end goal, which is the seller with the money in their pocket and you moved in to your first home.

I'll share with you the real-life things that you should be worried about, with ways to actively fix problems during the conveyancing process that can work no matter which conveyancing firm you choose to work with.

As a first-time buyer you are likely to be purchasing a leasehold flat, or buying through an affordable housing scheme, so I'll include guidance on the slight differences in the process.

We'll cover the complete conveyancing process in 8 stages

(*Chapters 3 to 10*), and I've also included a starter section called "How to save a Big enough Deposit to buy a house". In this section I'll explain how to save up for a deposit, with tips on how to find a property and secure it at the best possible price. If you've already found your first property to buy, then you can skip to *Chapter 3 – Instruct a Solicitor*. If your transaction falls through (1 in 3 do[1]), flick back *Chapter 2 - How to structure an offer on your new property*.

Scan the QR codes throughout the book with the camera on your smart device and it'll take you to more specialist tips, tools, calculators, and guides on the *SAM Conveyancing* website.

A few disclaimers

First off, the tag line of "without killing anyone" doesn't mean you would kill someone, should kill anyone, or that I intend to trivialise manslaughter. It means only that the process of buying a house can drive you mad, your stress levels can be pushed to the limit, and '*I could just kill them!*' is a figure of speech we hear a lot when the proverbial 'caca' hits the proverbial fan due to mismanaged expectations. I explain more in *Chapter 1 - Why does buying a house make you want to kill someone?*

This book is full of useful information which should be used to support and aid the process, but it does not substitute paid professional advice.

All data is correct at the time of writing unless otherwise stated. In the housing market things change, so make sure to get the up-to-date position from your professional advisors.

Sources are referenced and reputable, such as the Bank of

---

[1] https://www.homesellingexpert.co.uk/guides/what-percentage-of-house-sales-fall-through

England, Land Registry, and the Government. If you'd like to challenge any facts or data, I welcome constructive feedback at *help@samconveyancing.co.uk*

Please don't risk buying a property if you don't think you can afford to do it. A mortgage is a huge commitment and the decision to get a mortgage is not one to be taken lightly (the very word mortgage means death pledge in Old French), and your repayments can go up during the term of the mortgage. So, what you could afford early on, may become unaffordable as interest rates go up.

Whilst interest rates had been 2% or under since 2008, back in the 1980's interest rates were as high as 15%[2]. Base Rate has started increasing to combat the high inflation rates in 2022-3, which sees many homeowners who benefited from a low interest rate, now struggling to cover their mortgage repayments and living costs.

The ONS reported:

"The proportion of all adults finding it difficult (very or somewhat) to afford their energy bills, rent or mortgage payments has increased through the year, almost half of adults (45%) who paid energy bills (40% in March to June 2022) and 30% paying rent or mortgages reported these being difficult to afford (26% March to June 2022)"[3].

In addition to the stress and trauma of being unable to afford your bills, late payment or underpayment of bills could lead to your credit history being adversely affected and, in severe cases,

---

[2] https://www.bankofengland.co.uk/boeapps/database/Bank-Rate.asp

[3]
https://www.ons.gov.uk/peoplepopulationandcommunity/personalandhouseholdfinances/expenditure/articles/impactofincreasedcostoflivingonadultsacrossgreatbritain/junetoseptember2022

repossession (losing your home). This is why you must be realistic about whether you can afford to buy.

There is a big section in this book about mortgages. You need to know that **your home may be repossessed if you do not keep up with repayments of your mortgage.** Being repossessed means the bank takes over possession of your home and will sell it as quickly as possible for the highest price they can get, which is often well under the current market value. A quick sale almost always means a lower purchase price (this is why auctions are so popular, as you can pick up a repossession bargain).

Being repossessed effects your credit score, you could lose the deposit you paid to buy your home and still be in debt to your mortgage lender but be un-mortgageable due to your credit rating – meaning you can't remortgage the debt for a favourable rate. It can affect your physical and mental health and lead to PTSD. This is very serious, and I've included a section in *Chapter 10 – What happens if I can't afford to repay my mortgage?*

My advice is to speak to your mortgage lender the moment you are starting to struggle with the repayments on your mortgage. Do this as quickly as possible and let them see how they can help you[4].

If I give any advice or suggestions these should be viewed as tips only. I have no knowledge of your personal financial position. I don't know your own individual circumstances and my tips may not suit you. My suggestions are general and best practice. I do not provide financial advice.

I take no responsibility for the success, or failure, of any of the

---

[4] You can get free help and advice if you are in financial difficulty here:
https://www.citizensadvice.org.uk/debt-and-money/get-help-with-the-cost-of-living/
https://www.gov.uk/cost-of-living

practices in this book. The advice given is tried and tested, it usually works. But, in conveyancing, as in life, there are no guarantees.

The conveyancing process is full of jargon, so if you read a word and don't know what it means, flick to the back of the book and read the Glossary. It's all explained in plain English.

If you are looking for help buying your first home, then please reach out to my company *SAM Conveyancing*. You'll find a bunch of incredibly well trained and knowledgeable conveyancing gurus who can guide you through this process, with the support of our trusted panel solicitors, RICS surveyors and mortgage brokers. We hand select and introduce you to the best in the market to provide regulated services, then case manage the process from start to finish.

It's like having a personal shopper, except they'll tell you when that dress isn't flattering, or that extra price tag is unnecessary. Our clients call us a "concierge conveyancing service" and we're rated Excellent on Trustpilot.

CHAPTER 1

THE CONVEYANCING PROCESS EXPLAINED.

Why does buying a house make you want to kill someone?

According to the latest First Time Buyer Index research from specialist bank, Aldermore, over half of first-time buyers (52%[5]) were made ill with stress due to the complexity of house buying. On the Holmes-Rahe Life Stress Inventory, taking on a mortgage is ranked 20th.

In Maslow's hierarchy of needs[6], which is a motivational theory in psychology comprising a five-tier model of human needs, having shelter is the very basic need. Maslow asserted that so long as basic needs necessary for survival were met (e.g., food, water, shelter), higher-level needs (e.g., social needs) would begin to motivate behaviour.

The fear of having your home taken away, or losing your home to another buyer, can leave you unable to function and communicate as you normally would. When buying a house, you are left highly emotional and stressed because you are moving

---

[5] https://www.anxietyuk.org.uk/blog/risk-vs-reward-how-far-are-first-time-buyers-willing-to-go-to-get-on-the-property-ladder/
[6] https://www.simplypsychology.org/maslow.html

from one home to another, and you fear losing both.

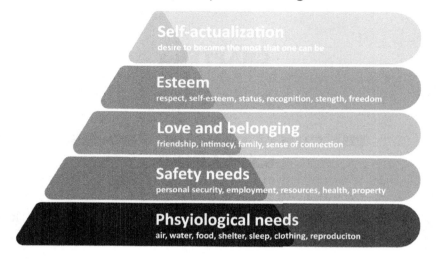

Whilst you're not going to murder someone, it is a description of how base level your reactions can get during the process. You might write a more aggressive email than you normally would do to your solicitor, or you might threaten to go to the seller's house and beat them up (both have been threatened, and more frequently than you think). Whilst these reactions are out of character, you are in a very difficult position, with limited control, wholly reliant on others to secure your base need of having a place to live.

These are intense human emotions which are often difficult to overcome, this book will help to combat your fears with:

1. **Good Communication** – always knowing what is going on; &
2. **Managing expectations** – always knowing what is happening next and when.

Armed with the above, you'll feel less reliant on others and more a part of the process. If at any point you feel out of control, turn to the relevant section in this book and it'll guide you on what to do.

Conveyancing Jargon

You can't get away from the fact that the legal system is complicated and full of jargon. Even 'Conveyancing'; such a weird word for buying a house. Flip to the back of the book to check out the glossary of terms, in plain English.

Who are the players in the game?

A standard sale and purchase can have up to 10 different people or companies involved. There's a lot of people in the game, so let's explain who each one is and what they do:

The buyer

This is you! After years of helping clients like you I know you will want to buy the property as quickly as possible with no issues. The rest of the book will deal with this so let's move on.

The seller

There are 6 different types of sellers, and each will influence the transaction both in length of time and complexity:

1. **Buying another property**. These sellers are selling their home to buy another one (they'll need to read my next book, "How to climb up the ladder without falling off", coming soon). For this type of transaction, you want to mirror the actions on your seller's onward purchase. For example, only order your searches when they order their searches.

You should always wait before paying for any searches or survey until you know your chain is complete i.e., the property your seller is buying isn't relying on another purchase to go through in order to become available. A complete chain has a seller at the top who isn't buying anything else – they are top of the chain. If you do spend out on searches, this money will be wasted if the chain isn't complete and the seller or the chain above them pull out because they can't find another property to buy.

Ask your estate agent to find out if the seller's offer is accepted and if the onward seller is buying anything else. Once you know the chain is complete and there is a top of the chain, then you can start spending money on searches and surveys.

The process is likely to last more than 12 weeks because of the number of people in the chain. We cover this in more detail in the next section – *What is a chain?*

2.   **Breaking the chain**. Whilst not a new concept, more sellers are choosing to move into rented housing and look to buy a new property 6 to 12 months later (often called "Chain Free" because your seller is top of the chain). The seller benefits because they aren't pressured by anyone else's time frames, and you enjoy a much shorter chain that can complete quicker (roughly 2 to 3 months for a house or 3 to 4 months for a flat).

What you need to watch out for, is when the seller finds a property they want to buy. This puts you into a chain, like the above, and timescales are then unpredictable until you know the position of everyone in the chain.

If the seller is serious about breaking the chain, try and find out if they have a rented or temporary property lined up and when this is going to be free for them to move into. Try and find out from the estate agent or ask the seller directly during the viewing.

3.   **Buy to let**. Where a landlord is selling a buy to let, they'll often want to complete as soon as possible. You should find out if the tenant has left the property. If they haven't, when were the tenants served notice to vacate the property? Does this tie in with when your rental agreement expires?

You can't exchange contracts until the tenant has moved out, so make sure to organise a viewing after they move out to inspect the property. Tenants often cause damage and leave possessions behind, so you'll want the landlord to address this prior to exchange.

Ideally your exchange will happen after the property is vacant so if you've got 2 months to wait then you're in for a smooth ride. If the property *is* vacant, expect the seller to pressure you for a quick transaction.

If you do exchange whilst the tenant is in the property, make sure that your solicitor makes your contract conditional on the seller giving vacant possession. You will also want to ensure that there is provision in the contract for you, the buyer, to exit (rescind) the contract, without losing your deposit and without penalties, if the tenant does not move out when expected, or if the property is damaged by the Tenants.

4.   **Probate**. This means the seller has passed away and the property is being sold by the Executors/Administrators. You need to find out if the Executors have obtained a Grant of Probate where the seller had a Will, or Letters of Administration where the seller died without a Will (this is the permission needed to sell the property). If they do not have a Grant and are required to obtain one, please beware. Following Covid there is a huge backlog at the Courts and the process could be delayed for months. You can't exchange until your solicitor has been supplied with a copy of the Grant because they need to know the executors or administrators have the legal right to sell the property. Without probate, they can't.

A probate sale property is often "sold as seen" in that any questions you may have about the property, such as "has it been flooded or been affected by subsidence", can't be answered by the seller, as they've most likely not lived in the property. Many answers the seller would usually supply about the property will be missing. You need to rely on your own investigations to make an informed decision around risks with any probate[7] property.

A probate sale often takes more than 3 months due to the issues around the grant of probate and delays with enquiries.

5.   **Care home**. The seller has moved into a care home which could lead to a probate sale. You may find the seller has someone looking after their affairs, who perhaps has a legal right to do so by reference to a Power of Attorney. If the seller is selling by their Attorney, your solicitor will need a copy of the Lasting Power of Attorney document which has been certified on every page.

As with a grant of probate, if the seller has a power of attorney expect to see a large amount of N/a in the Property Information Forms and be prepared to do your own investigations.

The time scales will be like a probate sale, at around 3 months or more.

6.   **New build developer**. When buying a new build, the seller is the top of the chain, but as a developer who has had a huge cash outlay to build the property, they'll want to exchange fast. Generally, you'll have to pay a non-refundable deposit to reserve the property and agree to exchange 28-56 days later.

Don't be too worried about the deadline set by the developer's selling agent. The timeframes often slip which is often caused by the seller's solicitor not being able to issue contracts or reply to enquiries in the set time. The most important thing is that you are proactive with getting your mortgage and ordering searches, so

---

[7] Find out more here: https://www.samconveyancing.co.uk/news/probate/probate-sale-top-tips-for-buyers-and-sellers-3771

that the developer and estate agent can see that you are well progressed, with only a few things left to do if you are running close to the wire.

Take some comfort from knowing that most new build exchange deadlines overrun, and this is accepted by the developer if you are actively moving the matter forward to exchange of contracts and not intentionally delaying the exchange to suit your own needs.

Beware direct communication with the seller!

I'm a huge fan of sellers and buyers genuinely working together to get to exchange. With a big BUT! Don't make the mistake of thinking that the seller is your mate, or that they are doing you a favour. Most sellers are simply looking to sell the property for the most amount of money as quickly as possible, whatever way they dress it up.

Most contracts will include a provision that you are not able to rely on any information given to you from the seller or any other third party directly unless it has been confirmed via the seller's solicitor. If you are in direct communication with the seller, then you should double check everything that is stated by the seller with your own solicitor. Your solicitor can then communicate this with the seller's solicitor, to ensure that its confirmed and incorporated into the information provided within the transaction.

These are just a few examples of issues that arise when sellers and buyers talk:

- *Seller informs you they'll throw in the fridge as part of the purchase.* You forget to pass this information onto your solicitor, it isn't included in the Fittings and Contents Form and the seller fails to leave the fridge in the property. You are left trying to sue the seller over a verbal agreement, which is very hard to prove. It should have been either noted in the contract of sale or an updated Fittings and Contents

Form.

- *Seller informs you that your solicitor has everything they need and asks why the process is stalling*? The seller may well have provided the information to their solicitor, but they don't know what your solicitor has done and what they are waiting for, because the seller's solicitor may not have made their client aware of this yet.

- *The seller informs you that they are breaking the chain*. You subsequently find out they are buying another property and want to link it to this chain.

If you are told anything by the seller, the best advice is to email this to your solicitor so that they can decide whether it needs to be written into the legal documentation for the purchase of the property.

Seller's solicitor
The seller's solicitor acts for the seller, and you cannot communicate directly with them – even though at times you may want to. The key role of the seller's solicitor is to:

1. Issue the draft contracts with supporting documentation;
2. Reply to enquiries;
3. Handle exchange; and
4. Receive completion monies, pay off the seller's mortgage and send the net sale proceeds to the seller.

I explain what can delay this process and leave you waiting on the seller's solicitor, in *Chapter 7 - What's the delay with draft contracts?* and *What are reasonable times to wait for stuff to get done?*

A challenge can arise if the seller uses a solicitor from a "Conveyancing Warehouse" or "Conveyancing Farm" where the service is notoriously slow, with poor client feedback. There is very little you can do about this other than be aware from the outset when you receive the Sales Memorandum. Google the reviews of the law firm used by the seller and see what their clients say about their service.

What is important to note is that you cannot communicate with the seller's solicitor under any circumstances, as they act for their client and cannot speak directly to you (their professional rules of conduct prohibit this). Plus, you cannot make a formal complaint about the service provided by the seller's solicitor as they aren't acting for you. Only the seller can complain about the service of their own solicitor.

If you try to get in contact with the seller's solicitor, they will contact your solicitor to advise you not to contact them again (don't take this personally).

Estate Agent
Since Purplebricks has entered the market there are now two very different types of estate agents, the local high street agent, and the online agent. As the buyer, you have no control over who sells the property on behalf of the seller, so you need to be aware of the different experiences that you can expect from either type:

A. *Local or 'high street' agent*
I'm a huge fan of high street estate agents when it comes to selling a property for the seller. They are trained professionals with experience of the local market. Some of the key roles the agent will play include:

1. Taking pictures of the property
2. Taking measurements for the floorplan
3. Setting the sale price with the seller
4. Handling viewings with potential buyers
5. Passing on all buyer's offers to the seller – (We'll look at

How to make a winning offer in *Chapter 2)*
6. Issuing the memorandum of sale
7. Case progression

My affection for the local high street estate agent stops at point 6 unless the estate agent employs a case progressor with years of experience. All too often I have seen an inexperienced case progressor or negotiator hyper-focused on reaching exchange and not focused enough on addressing any legal blockage preventing the buyer from proceeding. Many buyers have been pressured by the estate agent, into a purchase that should have been renegotiated, against their own legal advisor's better judgement.

I have experienced this time and time again. It's demoralising for a solicitor (they really do have their own client's best interest at heart) when the buyer starts believing only what the seller's agent is telling them, over their own solicitor.

There is a gap between the skill sets of an estate agent and a conveyancing solicitor when it comes to the nuances of resolving various risks to the buyer during legal enquiries. Estate agents simply don't have the legal savvy to understand the need for delay, and often hurry the transaction along to the buyer's detriment. For a solicitor it takes years to become conversant in the best way to handle conveyancing issues along the way.

I cover a wide variety of the most common issues that crop up in the legal enquiries raised by your solicitor in *Chapter 7 - How bad is the enquiry and should I be worried?*

B. *Online agent*
Purplebricks and other online agents have really shaken up the affordable online selling market. I think it is great that a seller can:

✓ List their own property.
✓ Take their own photos.

How To Buy a House Without Killing Anyone

✓ Handle their own viewings.
✓ Pay a cheaper fixed fee that isn't a % of the sale price.

What the online agent lacks though, is:

✗ A list of local buyers to cross sell the property to, although tools are in place to sell properties to registered buyers.
✗ Support in negotiations.
✗ Reliance on your own endeavours to sell through other estate agents. I've seen clients bound by the fixed fee even though they've had to sell through another agent in the future.

I still think the online selling experience is a huge win for a lot of sellers. In my opinion it is like the choice between flying budget versus premium airline (the local agent).

Take any update from the agent with a pinch of salt.
I promise I'm not an estate agent hater. I believe that a knowledgeable estate agent can have such a strong influence on the chain and can support getting to exchange. The challenge arises with the less-than-genuine estate agents, who use phrases such as:

• *"My seller has a higher offer, we need to exchange by Friday"* Really, if that is the case then why doesn't the seller accept that offer? Does the seller not like extra money?

• *"We've got viewings and they are very keen"*. Ok, have they offered?

If, at any stage, you feel pressurised by the estate agent, and hear this type of phrase:

"If you don't complete by the end of the month the seller will pull out".

Flag these to your solicitor directly. The seller and estate agents often get frustrated if there is an issue that is holding up an exchange. The best advice is communicating the blockage (unanswered legal enquiry) to the estate agent, and they'll pass this onto the seller. It is normally the seller who needs to answer the enquiry, so the sooner they are chased, the better. It diverts the attention away from you and onto the actual blockage.

In reply to such pressurising tactics, feel free to use this response that we often use at SAM Conveyancing, to protect our clients:

Hi [Estate Agent Name],

Thank you for your update, I appreciate we all want to get the completion through.

I'm sure you'll appreciate that there is a need to follow certain protocol and risk checks, as part of the solicitor's due diligence. I understand we are waiting for: XXX

I am aware we'd all like to get on to exchange, however I'm sure the seller would much prefer completing in just a few weeks, to having to wait to find a new buyer and start the process all over again, only for that buyer to come up against the same issue. A few weeks wait for me versus 4 to 6 months for a new buyer.

I suggest we focus on this chain and getting the above addressed as soon as possible.

Thank you for your help and support in getting this resolved.

This email aligns expectations and sets out what is needed by the seller to move on. It also sets a stake in the ground showing that you know it is in every one's interest to find the solution to the blockage and move on.

We will delve in deeper to other ways to help you communicate during the process in *Chapter 7 - What is the most efficient way to communicate during the purchase?*

Mortgage Broker

"A good mortgage broker is worth their weight in gold!"

I remember how happy I felt the first time I was approved for a mortgage, because in my eyes it was the hardest thing I had to do. It relies so much on a decision you have little control over (other than having a clean credit history and a massive deposit). Having a mortgage broker made that stress so much easier – Thank you Arvin Ramtuhul (my first mortgage broker back in 2001), sorry for being a stress-head, but I didn't have this book back then.

There are so many hurdles between you and your mortgage offer, having a trained professional mortgage broker to guide you is incredibly helpful. Although, you can get a mortgage direct from the lender without having a mortgage broker.

Some of the key benefits of using a mortgage broker are that they:

✓ have access to the whole mortgage market and not just the one mortgage lender's products.

✓ have access to mortgage products that mortgage lenders don't offer to clients who apply directly.

✓ provide options of a select few lenders that suit your circumstances.

✓ handle the mortgage application process (you do the form

filling; they'll handle the application directly with the lender for you).

✓ Obtain from you any additional information the lender requests for your mortgage application.

✓ Advise you against applying for unsuitable mortgage products (failed applications may damage your credit rating).

A mortgage broker needs to be regulated by the Financial Conduct Authority (FCA) to provide mortgage advice.

Mortgage brokers are paid:

1)   by you, upon application for your mortgage, although some waive this fee depending on the type of mortgage product you go for. The cost ranges from £100 to £500; and/or

2)   by the mortgage lender, on commission for your custom. If you ever want to know how much your mortgage broker got paid for the mortgage product you chose, look in your mortgage offer; either *Section 2 Credit intermediary* or *Section 13 Additional Information*. This ranges in line with the value of the product IE the broker gets paid more based on the size of the mortgage, the higher the interest and the longer the term.

The reason there is an application fee is to make sure they still get paid for their work, even if you don't get your mortgage, or choose to shop around. If there is an application fee (1 above) then why don't you ask for this to be refunded from the fee the broker makes from the mortgage lender (2 above) once you complete? The broker should agree, as they'll know they get to keep the upfront fee if you leave and they'll get their commission from the lender, if you complete.

Go direct or use a Mortgage Broker

This is a personal choice. I've always used a mortgage broker because I like to know that I have someone between me and the lender, who knows the process and can help when there is a problem. I like how the mortgage broker handles my mortgage application; they explain what additional information is needed, warn of potential blockages or delays, and I get to chase them to see how my application is going.

You may find that if you have bespoke circumstances, such as being self-employed, have income from multiple sources or are a non-UK resident, that a mortgage broker will be better placed to match your profile of mortgage application with a suitable lender as well as tell you what evidence the lender will need and in what format.

If you do go direct to a mortgage lender, make sure to apply to one lender at a time, as multiple applications may negatively influence your credit score.

You may find, by working directly with a bank, that you can find a suitable product by yourself, or that their services suit your needs because you already hold an account with them. Plus, you won't have to pay a mortgage application fee to your broker.

Whatever the reason, most mortgage lenders are in the business to lend to low-risk borrowers. So, if you have:

- ✓ Big enough deposit;
- ✓ Big enough income;
- ✓ Good credit score; and
- ✓ Good affordability.

Then you are the type of client they want to lend money to, regardless of whether you apply direct or go through a mortgage broker.

Valuers

Looking ahead to the next player in the game, you'll note that I have split up the two most common surveyors you'll be working with during your house purchase:

1)   *A mortgage valuer*, who acts for the mortgage lender to value the property and flag any issues that affect the value of the property (such as concrete build or subsidence); and

2)   *An independent RICS surveyor*, who acts for you, to provide an opinion on the defects within the property and their cost to you (more on defects later).

A mortgage valuer is instructed by the mortgage lender to value your property once you have successfully received a mortgage in principle. An offer in principle is a simple way to find out if you can borrow the amount you need to buy a property, usually without a full credit check.

Independent RICS Surveyor

Hiring an independent RICS surveyor isn't a mandatory part of the conveyancing process, but I would never buy a property without one.

You can choose any surveyor you like; you can find one through:

1) *Estate Agent Referral.* I've never understood why you would use a RICS surveyor suggested by the selling agent because it isn't in their interest for any defects to be found in the property, so their referral cannot be impartial. Yet, many clients do.

You may find that the estate agent has a referral fee for introducing you to a surveyor, make sure to ask if this is the case. This fee makes this type of referral more costly than finding a RICS surveyor through other channels.

2) *Online Search.* You can Google "Home Buyer Survey in London" or "Level 3 Building Survey in Newcastle" and you'll be greeted by a variety of different RICS surveyors in your local area where you can obtain quotes.

At SAM Conveyancing we speak to a lot of clients looking for independent surveys which is why we have local surveyors throughout England and Wales. I find as a tip, when doing a search like this, the best survey providers will:

a) Review the property you're buying and make sure you choose the right level of survey for your property (there are 3 Levels).

b) Have good availability (not more than 5 to 7 working days – although busier times mean a longer wait, such as bank holidays, August when most surveyors have a long holiday, Easter, and Christmas).

c) Are RICS qualified – AssocRICS, MRICS or FRICS. There are other surveyor qualifications but these 3 are the only ones who can provide RICS templated reports.

d) Give you a call on the day to provide an appraisal of the property.

Naturally, we do all the above at *SAM Conveyancing*[8].

3) *Referral from family or friends.* A good surveyor is like a good mortgage broker, once you have one, you tell your friends and family about them. Make sure to ask for any personal referrals and then look at their quotes, reviews, and availability.

---

[8] Get a Free Home Survey appraisal - https://www.samconveyancing.co.uk/Homebuyers-Survey

Is a mortgage valuation a defect survey?

The mortgage valuation is conducted by a surveyor instructed by the mortgage lender of their choosing. It's important to remember that the Mortgage Valuation is a report which is purely for the lender's purposes in accordance with the Mortgage Valuation Guidelines issued by the Royal Institution of Chartered Surveyors and the guidelines they issue to their Valuers. This does not meet RICS guidelines for any of the Survey products they offer (such as the Level 2 Home Survey or the Level 3 Building Survey) and is unsuitable for use by you.

Understanding the difference between a Valuation and a Survey is important. For example, Valuers do not enter sub-floor, roof, or similar voids, move obstructions, floor coverings, or examine or test services such as gas, electrical drains, and heating. The Valuer doesn't make enquiries, like your solicitor would. Your solicitor and independent surveyor need to check for defects themselves and your solicitor should report anything that could affect the mortgage valuers Valuation.

You can't assume that if your mortgage lender offers you a mortgage, that the property doesn't have any defects. The mortgage valuer and lender wash their hands with the risk on this and do not accept any responsibility or liability to you or other parties in connection with the Valuation report even if the report contains errors, omissions, or inaccuracies.

It is for the above reason that you should instruct your own RICS surveyor to undertake either a Level 2 or Level 3 Home Survey to highlight any potential visual defects with the property.

Local Authority

Your solicitor will obtain a local authority search from the local authority. This is one of the 4 main searches you'll need during the conveyancing process, which include:

- ✓ Local Authority Search
- ✓ Water and Drainage Search
- ✓ Environmental Search
- ✓ Chancel Search

Depending on the location of your property there are other searches to consider, such as coal mining, tin mining etc.

A local authority search can take upward of 8 weeks to be sent by the local authority; some take only a few days. Your solicitor will advise you on the length of time that the Council local to the property will take to send you this search.

Your solicitor will either apply for the local search direct from the council, known as an official search, or they'll instruct a search agent, known as a regulated search. The former is normally more expensive than the latter. I explain this more in *Chapter 6 - Conveyancing searches.*

Water Board
Your solicitor orders the water and drainage search from the water board that supplies the property you intend to purchase.

The search can take upwards of 2 weeks to be returned and there is either an official search, or a regulated search.

Environment agency
The environmental search is the fastest search to come back during the process. It can be returned 1 working day after the solicitor orders it, although it is normally within hours.

Freeholder
If you are buying a leasehold property, then the freeholder

needs to provide information to the seller's solicitor, to pass on to the buyer's solicitor. This is because the freehold owns the main structure of the building and the land that the building sits upon; sometimes the freeholder will use a management company (see below) to handle the obligations of the freeholder, in which case it will be the management company that will provide the necessary information to the seller, to provide to your solicitor.

The information is often slow to be sent through (3 to 6 weeks) and can often be incomplete, resulting in further information requests.

Freeholders and/or their management companies are the prime cause for leasehold purchases taking longer to complete than freeholds.

Management Company

If the property you are buying is leasehold, a management company usually handles the obligations of the freeholder, such as collecting ground rent and service charges. On new build developments (even if built some years ago), where there are common parts, such as a private road, landscaped areas, or shared facilities, it is usual for a management company to oversee the collection of service charges for repair and maintenance, etc. of the common parts.

There is normally only one managing company, however you can encounter leaseholds where there is a management company to collect service charges and handle the maintenance obligations and then there is a freehold management company that handles the collection of the ground rent. Where there are two managing agents expect there to be a much longer conveyancing process, well over 12 weeks.

A word on ground rent: Yes, you do have to pay rent on a property you've bought. When buying a leasehold, you pay rent on the 'ground' the property is built on, as that belongs to the freehold. Thankfully, new legislation means this is capped at one peppercorn per year for new leases. Literally - salt and pepper. A peppercorn was chosen specifically because it's not valuable - it needed to be a nominal sum, but 'something' must be due each year, to establish a rental arrangement. So, get your pepper mill out and pay up!

What is a chain?

A chain[9] is the name for linked transactions, with each buyer or seller in the middle relying on their sale to proceed, for their purchase to proceed, for a full chain to be completed. Knowing who is in your chain is one of the most important parts of the conveyancing process and can help you to manage your expectations.

As we've seen above, there are so many people involved in just the purchase of the property so when you add a seller, as well as their onward purchase, you can end up with 30 parties involved and any one of them could be the cause of a delay to your own exchange and completion.

Here are 4 examples of what chains could look like:

1) Buyer > Seller.
   2 people in the chain is easier – often called "Chain Free".

2) Buyer > Selling & Buying > Seller.
   3 people – Normal.

3) Buyer > Selling & Buying > Selling & Buying > Seller.

---

[9] Download a FREE Chain Checklist -
https://www.samconveyancing.co.uk/news/conveyancing/how-does-a-property-chain-work-5146

4 people – Harder.

4) Buyer > Selling & Buying > Selling & Buying > Selling & Buying > Seller.
   5 people – Nightmare.

Chain Checklist

	1st in chain	2nd in chain	3rd in chain	Top of chain
What is the address of the property?	N/a			
When would they like to complete by?*				
Who is the selling estate agent? (name & email)	N/a			
Are they getting a mortgage?				N/a
Could they break the chain if they had to?				N/a

* Completion dates are only estimates and are likely to change.

These are just examples, looking at them you'll probably assume a chain free purchase will complete faster than a chain with 5 people in it. This is a fair assumption; but incorrect, because it isn't just the number of sellers and buyers in a chain that is the sole cause for delays and issues. I've seen chains with 5 sellers and buyers complete in 8 weeks, whereas a supposed chain free purchase took 6 months because the buyer was so fixated on it being chain free, they forgot that about everything else.

What do you need to find out about your chain?

When you look at your chain, you need to look past how many sellers and buyers there are and drill more into the following:

1) *Who is at the top of the chain?* It can only be one of the 6 types we listed in *Chapter 1 – The Seller* and if it's a probate sale or the seller is moving into a care home then as chain free as the transaction is, there is no amount of pressure or chasing that you can do that'll move the process on any faster.

2) What date does the chain have in mind for completion? You might want 8 weeks; others might want 12 weeks because that's when their early mortgage redemption charge expires. (An Early Mortgage Redemption Charge, or EMRC, is where a party wishes to sell a property and pay off their mortgage before the end of a fixed rate period – this often costs them additional charges for repaying early).

What can you do to speed up your chain?

- ✓ Choose a solicitor with good capacity who uses technology effectively.
- ✓ Get your mortgage application in as soon as possible.
- ✓ Order searches and survey when you know your seller is ordering theirs but beware if the chain isn't complete.

Sometimes you can do everything right and still you're stuck with a slow purchase because someone in the chain isn't as driven as you. Whilst it'll be annoying, there's nothing you can do to change this other than keep updated through your estate agent and solicitor.

What's different when buying a new build?

Whether you are buying under an affordable housing scheme or you are buying direct from the developer, if you are a first-time buyer then the process is as follows:

1) Find a property and pay a reservation deposit.
2) Agree to exchange within 28 – 56 days.
3) Completion, either at an estimated date in the future, or straight away because the property is built.

The best new build transactions are the ones where the property has already been built and is ready to move into. The worst ones are those with an estimated completion date that is 5 to 6 months in the future (or even a year). If you are getting a mortgage, you need a formal mortgage offer before you can exchange. As we've seen, mortgage offers only last for 6 months. While some lenders allow an extension of time on the offer, others do not.

Where you exchange on a new build with a valid mortgage offer, but the developer takes longer than 6 months to build the property, your offer will expire. Delays are common, so whilst you may have a mortgage offer that falls within the expiration date, the actual completion date could move by months, thus your offer will expire, and you'll need a new one. If you are unable to get a new mortgage offer for any reason, you won't be able to buy the property.

If you can't obtain a new mortgage offer, the worst-case scenario will be that you lose your 10% deposit and pay the costs of the developer's solicitor. The best-case scenario is that you find a mortgage provider to give you a different mortgage  offer in time for completion. The challenge to this is that you only have a few working days from notice to complete, usually 7, 10 or

14 days[10].

Why does it take so long?

You have heard about chains, probate sales, developer deadlines and the general faff of how solicitors work. Add to these other factors, such as struggling to get a mortgage, major events like COVID, or Government budgets around stamp duty, then add real-life sickness, holidays and finally, slow, or overworked solicitors.

The conveyancing process has been screaming to be updated, from faxes and original documents to digital signatures and streamlined solicitor practices. The light at the end of the tunnel is very close, as the Land Registry have pledged to make the conveyancing process for deeds digital... at some point in the future.

This is a huge step forward, but until solicitors start working in an equally streamlined digital manner then we will still see an average time of 3 months to get to exchange for freehold and upward for leaseholds.

What can you do to speed it up?

There are ways to speed up the conveyancing process and I've seen many clients successfully make this work, on the back of my advice. There is a huge caveat here though. There is no magic wand to make this happen, because so much of the process is reliant on factors outside of your control.

Throughout this book I'll flag time-saving solutions for a wide variety of issues that crop up. The majority of these can be found in *Chapter 7 – Contracts and Enquiries*.

---

[10] https://www.samconveyancing.co.uk/news/conveyancing/can-i-pull-out-after-exchange-of-contracts-370

What are the different types of affordable housing?

There are affordable housing options to help lower income households get onto the housing market. Whilst I'll refer to some of the differences in the process below, here are some of the criteria and key differences to the process for each.

Shared Ownership

This is a part rent, part buy scheme. You can either buy a new build or a resale (meaning it was previously owned). The property always has a lease over it even if it is a house. The first share you buy is between 10% and 75% of the home's full market value.

You can take out a mortgage to buy your share or pay for it with savings. You'll also need to pay a deposit, usually between 5% and 10% of the share you're buying.

You can buy more shares in your home in the future. This is known as 'staircasing'. If you buy more shares, you'll pay less rent. The amount of rent you pay will be based on the landlord's share.

Right to Buy

You can buy your Council House which you have rented, at a discount, subject to certain criteria being met.

The main difference in the process is that you don't exchange contracts which isn't such an issue because you're already living in the property. What you do need to factor in though, is that it takes 4 to 6 months to complete, as the council are very slow.

Rent to Buy

You can rent a property at a subsidised rate, helping you to save up a deposit to buy it in the future. This must be a certain type of rental, i.e., you can't just buy your landlord's house because you would like to!

CHAPTER 2

HOW TO GET YOUR OFFER ACCEPTED

What can you afford?

The very first thing to do before even looking for a property is to work out how much you can afford. Otherwise, it is like window shopping in Louis Vuitton. Now, I'm not saying it isn't a good idea to keep an eye on the local market for what you think you can afford; just don't progress with viewings or offers without crunching the numbers. Most good estate agents won't put your offer forward until they know what you can afford.

Working out what you can afford is easier than you think. Here is a very simple table you can use to work out the price of the property you can afford to buy:

What is your deposit?	£50,000
(Include gifts from family)	
What is your last year's gross annual income? (What appeared on your P60 last year or SA302 self-assessment tax form last year)	
Applicant 1	£25,000
Applicant 2	£30,000
Total	£55,000

What mortgage can you get?	£247,500
(Salary multiple for mortgage @ 4.5)	

What property value can you go up to?	£297,500
(Deposit plus mortgage)	

This is an example. Yours will be different and the mortgage multiples aren't always 4.5 (it ranges from 3 to 5). The 2 key metrics which effect the value of the property you can buy are:

1) How big is your deposit?
2) How big is your salary?

Bigger is definitely better in both cases and there is one other metric which now plays a factor which is: What do you spend your money on?

We cover all of these in more detail along with other complications for Non-Resident and self-employed borrowers in *Section 4 – How are you financing the purchase?*

How to save a 'big enough' deposit
Saving for your deposit is one of the hardest and longest parts of the conveyancing process and the goal posts keep being moved as property prices rise.

In 2015 I wrote a book – *How long before you'll never be able to buy a property?*[11] and whilst it sounds sensational, let me show you why for so many people, this is now a reality:

---

[11] You can buy it from Amazon for £1.99 - https://www.amazon.com/long-before-youll-never-house-ebook/dp/B00QE35MVE

"In 1971 the average house cost £5,632 where now it's £260,000 – a 4,616% increase. If shop prices had gone up at the same rate, a 23p carton of milk would cost £10.62 today and a 9p loaf of bread would be £4.15."

The average house price in England and Wales is now £294,910 (November 2022) and is the highest it has ever been.

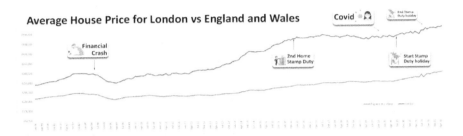

There's always talk of a property crash that'll make property prices fall and this may still happen. However, as you can see from the graph above, house prices have not fallen for any length of time, except for the financial crash in September 2007 - from which they did recover in the long run.

For most mortgage lenders, you'll need a minimum of a 10% deposit. Buy to let landlords will require a minimum of 25%. The best mortgage interest rates are where you can invest 40% or more deposit. But, as a first-time buyer, it'll take years to save up 40% without a gift from friends or family.

Here's an example:

For an average priced house of £295,000 (April 2022) you'll need a £29,500 deposit. If you were able to save £200 a month then in just over 12 years, you'll have enough money to buy your first home. Annoyingly though, in 12 years the average house price is most likely going to be £350,000 to £400,000. Therefore, getting on the property ladder sooner rather than later means you'll need a smaller deposit.

There are affordable housing schemes. such as Shared Ownership, where you pay a 10% deposit on your share of the property. For example, if you are getting a 25% share in a property valued at £295,000 then your 10% deposit is £7,375 (£295,000 * 25% = £73,750 * 10%). Saving £200 a month it'll take 3 years. This presents a much shorter and more affordable solution for buying your first home, although it comes with its downsides, which we cover in *Chapter 2 – Affordable Housing*.

You may be fortunate enough (although the bereavement itself is unfortunate) to inherit money or be gifted cash toward your deposit, which can reduce the time. The latter is incredibly common and according to a survey commissioned by Legal & General[12] 56% of those buying their first home did so using a gift from family or friends.

Whilst a gift is common, you'll need to declare the gift to your mortgage lender and your solicitor will require additional information around proof of funds and a gift declaration[13]. I will explain how to prove the source of funds for a gift in *Chapter 4 – How to prove source of funds*.

Share buying with a friend, family member or companies.
We call this 'share a mortgage' and there are many mortgage lenders who offer mortgage products that allow friends or family to join up and apply for a mortgage together. Here are a few examples:

- **Joint Mortgage Sole Proprietor**. This is a specific mortgage

---

product that allows a friend or a family member to use their income to strengthen your salary multiple, to get a larger mortgage, but they aren't named on the legal title. Like a guarantor mortgage, there is huge risk for the party who isn't on the legal title, so they need independent legal advice. They'll also need a deed of trust to affirm that they have no beneficial interest in the property, which will mean they won't attract the additional rate of stamp duty. Lenders such as Barclays and HSBC offer this product.

- **Guarantor mortgage**. A guarantor mortgage, or family assist mortgage, is a type of mortgage, or home loan, where a 'guarantor' (usually a parent or older relative) shares the risk of the mortgage by agreeing to take on some of the liability for the loan.

- **Share a Mortgage**. This is where friends or flat mates join forces and buy a property together using their joint deposit and salaries to make buying a property affordable.

In my opinion, with rising house prices and a generation of homeowners who rent, the support of parents or friends who are already on the ladder to support first time buyers is going to continue. *shareamortgage.com* sets out the different ways to share a mortgage.

How to find a property to buy

"If you think that you find your new home on Rightmove or Zoopla then you are wrong."

There, I've said it, and I want to be clear on why this isn't the case. It isn't that your new home won't end up on the internet at some point because it probably will. What most people don't know is that any high street estate agent has had a property offline for up to 2 weeks, which means by the time it hits the internet on Rightmove or Zoopla, that seller has probably had 20 viewings and an open day.

Why? Because savvy estate agents must pay to list on these online platforms, so they save money by advertising to their portfolio of buyers first, of whom they already know which are looking for this type of property.

Here are my steps to finding a house to buy:

1) Choose the area you want to buy in using a Rightmove or Zoopla search to ascertain current average sale prices. This is good research and could save you a lot of time choosing a location outside of your price bracket.

2) Go into all the local offices for those estate agents within that local area. Yes, all of them. Meet the sales negotiator who will find your first home in person. Tell them what you can afford (not your maximum budget, keep that to yourself to use in negotiations if you need to), give them some details around your deposit and your mortgage affordability.

3) Ring round once a week and keep yourself front of mind to each estate agent.

4) Make sure you are on the estate agent's email/postal list, for when the property which may fit your requirements and profile comes to market.

How do you make an offer to the seller?

"I'm going to make you an offer you can't refuse."
Marlon Brando, Godfather Part I

This part of the book will save you every penny you spent on it, because it is all about the offer you make to the seller to buy their home. Doing this right can save you thousands of pounds. Doing it wrong could leave you paying more than you should, and powerless in the hands of the seller/estate agent.

Making an offer on a property you really want is nerve racking, but when you realise the seller and agent both need your offer just as much as you want the property, you are on a level playing field.

How do most first-time buyers get it wrong?

The biggest mistake when making an offer to an estate agent, is to make the Dragons' Den type of offer. For anyone who hasn't seen the BBC 1 show, this is where an entrepreneur stands in front of 5 clued up businesspeople with stacks of cash, and they say (normally with wobbly knees) "I'm looking for £100,000 for a 10% stake in my business". With no caveats, or time scales, or understanding that they have something of value, worth more than the money the Dragons have.

If the Dragons like the idea, they take control of the vulnerable entrepreneur and say, "*I'd like to make you an offer for all the money, but for more equity*". The entrepreneur can wrestle back control but should have put a better first offer in to make sure they don't get this push back and lose valuable equity. I never understand why the entrepreneur doesn't say "*I'm looking for £100,000 for 10% of my business, with this investment I will deliver this turnover by year one and I will pull my offer in 5 minutes if no one wants to invest. Now who has any questions*".

So how does this relate to a first-time buyer making an offer on a house? Everything, because in every type of negotiation you need to:

1) Be likeable and engaging to the other parties;

2) set a boundary that you control;

3) make an offer based on evidence;

4) set caveats to your offer that link to the needs of the seller; and

5) have a timeframe as to when your offer expires.

I've heard first-time buyers email an offer along the lines of "We love the property, and we want to make an offer for the full asking price of £295,000. Can you let us know as soon as possible if the seller accepts". If you did this, don't worry. You're reading this book and can try a different way to make a winning offer next time, where you retain some bargaining power.

The challenge with making an offer like the one above is that you have given up all your control and you're basically saying, "I'm emotionally attached to your home, I'll give you what you want, please let me know if I can have it...please!!!". You've lost ground, the estate agent will smell blood in the water and either now or in the future, they will use this against you.

Negotiating doesn't just get you the best purchase price, it also sets the tone that you won't be pushed around in the future. It says you are prepared to set a boundary and defend it. The real art is setting a boundary that allows the seller and the estate agent to win, all at the same time.

Sound too good to be true? Let's delve deeper into how you can do this by working out what each party at this negotiation table classes as a win. To do this we need to understand what each party needs (aside from just money).

What is a win for you?
Now I get that the simple answer is the property, for the lowest price possible. Have you considered that a win could also be:

✓ to complete a week before your tenancy ends;

✓ to complete before your mortgage offer expires;

✓ to complete in time to get into the school catchment area of the local school for the forthcoming year; and/or

✓ to get the white goods thrown in for free as part of the purchase price.

You should also consider that sellers are often worried when accepting offers from first-time buyers, as they worry you may struggle to get a formal mortgage offer. A high proportion of transactions fall through because of this issue, so having evidence to prove your mortgage affordability will put the seller's mind at rest.

What is a win for the seller?
Let's get the obvious one out the way, to sell the property for as much as possible. A win for them could be:

✓ to find a buyer after being on the market for months;

✓ to complete at the same time as their onward purchase, which could mean delaying their sale to you, or faster if they are buying a new build;

✓ to complete when they find a new property to buy because they've just lost their onward purchase; and/or

✓ to buy the property in a bad condition with no requests to do it up before completion.

The power a buyer has when they make an offer to the seller is all too often ignored. You can see this if you stand in the seller's shoes for a moment and ask the question: *how long was their property on the market for*?

You can easily find this out through researching the listing on Rightmove, it'll tell you when the property was first listed and how many times the property was reduced in price. The latter could mean the seller is already disappointed that their original hopes, often set by the estate agent, have been realigned to a much-reduced sale price.

After a month's worth of viewings or more, a seller will get fed up with keeping the property in great condition, for every single viewing that has been booked in that time. As a first-time buyer you won't have experienced this, but it is really hard work keeping the property "show room" ready in the hope the next viewing is going to be the one. In just one month a seller could have around 20 viewings, and that's 20 times where they'll hear: "*we love your home*", but the buyers don't put an offer in, or if they do it is so low it is disheartening.

It can be soul destroying; having so many people walk in your home and snub it by not offering what you and the estate agent think it is worth. Add to this the frustration of having found your perfect new home and then losing it, because you can't find a buyer for your old property.

It isn't plain sailing and sellers have it hard, so when you come along, you honestly fall in love with the property, and you make a Winning Offer, the seller will be over the moon to accept, (with a bit of toing and froing).

What is a win for the estate agent?
You could guess, but what the estate agent wants is:

✓ To complete the purchase as quickly as possible;

✓ For as much money as possible to maximise the fee they take for their commission, which usually equates to a.% of the selling price; and

✓ To complete and get the negotiator's share of the commission before their salary run for the month.

The issue estate agents have is that they can be let down by buyers who try and gazunder the seller (this is where a buyer offers a lower amount to their original offer, typically just before exchange) or who can't get a mortgage. Both factors are covered under *how to make a Winning Offer*.

Watch out for*:*

"I have an offer at asking, so if you go over asking, I'm sure you'll get it."

If I had a pound for every time a client has told me this is what they were informed. The estate agent shouldn't tell you about other offers, this ploy is there solely to get an offer over asking price, so that they make more commission.

"The seller won't accept that."

We come onto this later, and I'll explain how all offers must be presented to the seller.

So, how do I make an offer to the seller? We've seen the varying needs for all parties, now how on Earth do you make an offer that allows everyone to win? Here's how to make that winning offer.

How do you make a Winning Offer?

Now, before we start, there are zero guarantees this will work and for obvious reasons. You might put in an offer that makes sense to you, allows the seller and estate agent to win, but in the end, they still refuse for some personal reason. It is often pride but could simply be because your Winning Offer went up against a financially better one (cash buyer) or one where the agent feels they can better manoeuvre the buyer, toward a quicker, less questions purchase.

In these cases, you'll have dodged a bullet because buying the property would have meant removing or ignoring your boundaries, which could mean buying a property with a problem or hidden costs in the future.

I would add that it is also rare for a Winning Offer not to get through the standard Estate Agent replies of, "we have other offers, is this your best one?" or, "the seller isn't likely to accept this" or even, "that's too low, I won't even waste my seller's time".

A Winning Offer sets out what you feel will be a win for everyone, however the final price is still up for debate; you might end up conceding something or gaining something else for a different purchase price. This is fine and to be expected. By making and negotiating your offer in this way, you'll remain in control.

Start the negotiation off during the viewing.
This is absolutely one of the most important stages of the process. When the seller receives your offer, they'll remember Andrew from the viewing (tall, polite, smiling), over an email with a blanket offer. The seller will have the picture of you at the viewing and how they liked you, when they are thinking about your offer.

I have seen offers from a small family that are under asking price, beat those of a buy to let landlord, because the owner wanted their home, the home they raised their children in, to go to a new family. This means during your first viewing you need to:

   ✓   Be engaging;

✓ Love how they have made the property look (they've lived in it, so they like it);

✓ Ask the seller's opinions, such as which supermarket is closer, how busy is the road in the mornings, which are the best schools (ask if the one you're looking at is any good), even which is the best pub for food and drink. The seller is likely to have lived there for a number of years so will appreciate you asking their opinion;

✓ Break the ice by flattering obvious parts of the house you like such as good light, big windows, a south facing garden or easy parking. It is OK to show you are interested and it is important to show you really like the property;

✓ Dress to impress. First impressions are so important so treat it like an interview and look sharp;

✓ Chat about their journey so far and what they are doing next. Have they been on the market long, are they buying another property, do they have any time frames in mind. This is a great opportunity to chat and align expectations, to show you're a good fit if they accept your offer; and

✓ Before you enter the house always ask, "would you like me to take my shoes off". This shows you are well mannered and considerate. This is still their home, let them know you respect this by asking what the rules of the house are.

This of course relies upon you meeting with the seller during the viewing. If you don't, then ask similar questions of the selling agent to show you are interested in the property. Fewer questions mean there are fewer buying signals for the agent to pick up on, which they may interpret to mean that you're not seriously interested in buying the property.

Once again, it is ok to be really excited about the property and say *"I could really see us living here"* during the viewing, but how you phrase this in the offer email must be more levelled. **Lead with your head, not your heart.**

Summary of what you need to make a Winning Offer

Now you've done the viewing, love the house and want to make it your own. The first thing you need to do is get yourself ready to make an offer. This is what you will need (in order of time priority as some of these take longer to get than others):

✓ Get an initial mortgage illustration for what you can afford. Not a full-blown mortgage in principle, an illustration is an initial assessment of your affordability. You can get this from a mortgage broker or direct with a lender.

✓ Put together market research of 10 sold properties of the same size, in the same area (Sqm or Sqft) and work out the cost per Sqm/Sqft – Sold price divided by Sqm/Sqft = cost per Sqm/Sqft. Then times it by the Sqm/Sqft of your property. This is how RICS valuers provide their own valuations, so it'll be good enough for any estate agent and based on fact – although make sure the properties you use are local and on the same street. The results are best shown in a table like the one below[14], which you may copy or fill out in this book, to conduct your own research:

Property Address	Rightmove link	Sold for (£)	Date sold	Price per Sqm/Sqft

---

[14] Use our online calculator: https://www.samconveyancing.co.uk/house-offer-calculator

✓ Scan your evidence of proof of funds for your deposit. A snippet of your bank statement should suffice. I use the free Snipping Tool from Microsoft Store, so you can save just your bank balance showing the money in the account and not share anything else. For now, they just need to see you're good for the cash. The due diligence of checking where it came from takes place later, in *Chapter 3 – How to prove source of funds.*

✓ Scan your ID and proof of address to PDF.

✓ Instruct a solicitor to handle your conveyancing. Get the name, email, and direct dial of your solicitor.

Your first Winning Offer

Now you have all the information you need to make your winning offer; I want to list out the key components of what your offer email needs to include:

1) Be likeable and engaging to the other parties;
2) Set a boundary that you control;
3) Make an offer based on evidence;

4) Set caveats to your offer, that link to the needs of the seller; and
5) Have a timeframe as to when your offer expires.

Using everything we learned from our first viewing, estate agent and research this is an example offer:

Hi David,

Thank you so much for taking the time to take us round the property on Tuesday. Claudine and I loved how spacious the property was and could see ourselves making this a home for us.

We've crunched the numbers and we would like to make an offer of £250,000 which will include the white goods we discussed during the viewing.

We've based our offer on these comparables which we feel align with the market of the local area based on size and condition:

[Include your market research table]

We've attached our mortgage illustration as proof we can get a mortgage and we will make our formal mortgage application as soon as our offer is accepted.

We also attach our bank statement to evidence the deposit we are using.

To speed the process up I have instructed [Name of solicitor & firm] who are ready to go as soon as the sales memo is issued.

During the viewing, Jane and Michelle mentioned they haven't found a property to buy yet, and we are happy to wait and work with them until they find a property to buy.

We hope the above is acceptable and look forward to hearing from you by Friday or earlier. If you need anything else, then please let us know.

Kind regards,

Claudine and Andrew

Let's tick off the different parts of the Winning Offer:

- ✓ *Be likeable and engaging to the other parties* – spoke about the property, used the seller's name.

- ✓ *Set a boundary that you control* – include white goods, aware of the mortgage process, have a solicitor ready.

- ✓ *Make an offer based on evidence* – your offer, even if below asking price, is based on actual data. Expect the agent to negotiate on this part.

- ✓ *Set caveats to your offer that link to the needs of the seller* – happy to wait for them to find a buyer.

- ✓ *Have a timeframe as to when your offer expires* – there is no need at the first stage to state the offer will expire but confirm a day when you expect to hear back from the seller with their feedback.

You should never chase until the deadline you have set, as it shows you are too keen and could mean the estate agent will use this to push your offer up. The next move is the estate agents, so sit on your hands and wait for them to reply because no amount of chasing or pressure will speed up the response.

Can the estate agent...
Refuse to put my offer forward?

Under The Property Ombudsman Code of Practice for Residential Estate Agents – Section 9a[15], it states:

"By law, you must tell sellers as soon as is reasonably possible about all offers that you receive at any time until contracts have been exchanged unless the offer is an amount or type which the seller has specifically instructed you, in writing, not to pass on. You must confirm each offer in writing to the seller, and to the buyer who made it, within 2 working days."

If the estate agent refuses to put your offer to the seller, then you should quote the above, in an email, along these lines:

Hi Estate Agent,

Further to your email/call today, confirming that you will not put my offer dated the 30th of October 202X through to the seller as you feel the offer is too low, I'm writing to ask you to review this position. As you'll note under Clause 9a of The Property Ombudsman Code of Practice for Residential Estate Agents unless you have written instructions from the seller to not pass on offers of this value or type, then you'll be in breach of this code.

Please can you confirm that you have specific written authority from the seller, not to accept the offer I have put forward?

I look forward to hearing from you, either with confirmation that you have the above in writing from the seller, or, that you have now submitted my offer to the seller for their consideration, as I would very much like to move forward with the purchase of this property.

Although it is an uncomfortable conversation to have, so early

---

[15] https://www.tpos.co.uk/images/codes-of-practice/TPOE27-8_Code_of_Practice_for_Residential_Estate_Agents_A4_FINAL.pdf

on in negotiations, these are professional estate agents who shouldn't impede your ability to make an offer to the seller. Plus, if you have followed the process when putting together a Winning Offer, then your offer is based on facts, and so is a reasonable offer for the property.

Can an agent influence me on how I should proceed with the purchase?

Under The Property Ombudsman Code of Practice for Residential Estate Agents – Section 12a, it states:

"After acceptance of the offer by the seller, and until exchange of contracts you have no direct influence on such matters as the conveyancing process or the mortgage lending process. Your obligations to the client are:

- *to monitor progress;*
- *to assist where possible, as asked;*
- *to report information deemed helpful to bringing the transaction to fruition;*
- *where there is a chain, routinely check the immediate transactions and communicate information helpful to bringing your client's transaction to fruition.*

You must keep written or electronic records of such activity."

If your estate agent is trying to influence you by phone or email about how to progress with the transaction, you should flag this to the office manager at the estate agents. If it is the manager themselves, then raise a complaint to the Area Manager of the branch. If you can't stop the influence via this route, you can make a complaint under The Property Ombudsman (TPOS)[16].

---

[16] https://www.tpos.co.uk/consumers/how-to-make-a-complaint

Can an agent force me to use their preferred solicitor?

When your offer is accepted, it is time to instruct your solicitor. Most estate agents will suggest their preferred solicitor. Make sure you shop around and make your own decision about which solicitor is going to be the best option for you.

Under The Property Ombudsman Code of Practice for Residential Estate Agents – Section 18a, it states:

"Aggressive Behaviour. Here are some illustrative examples of aggressive behaviour or practices. It is not an exhaustive list. In each case, the test is whether the average consumer's freedom of choice or conduct is (or would be likely to be) impaired and, as a result, they take (or would be likely to take) a different transactional decision. When you gain new clients and instructions, when you market property, when you negotiate and make sales.

Pressuring a potential buyer to use associated services, for example to take out a mortgage through the in-house mortgage advisor or to use a particular firm of solicitors or licensed conveyancers."

And under Section 9d, it states:

"By law you cannot make it a condition of passing on offers to the seller that the buyer must use services offered by you or another party. You must not discriminate, or threaten to discriminate, against a buyer because that person declines to accept that you will (directly or indirectly) provide related services to them."

It is essential that you have the right to choose who you want to work with as your legal advisor, without any pressure from the estate agent.

What if they don't accept your offer?

When a seller rejects your first offer, or even a second offer, don't be despondent. You need to find out from the estate agent if there is anything else, other than the money side of the offer, that would make your offer more appealing.

✓ Does the seller want to leave items with the house, that you can buy?

✓ Does the seller want a specific completion date that you'll agree to?

✓ Would signing a non-refundable deposit agreement show your commitment to the purchase?

If it does just come down to the money, then be careful not to overstretch yourself. Whilst you may be able to afford the mortgage on paper, can your budget stretch to afford the costs each month along with all your other commitments?

Whatever you offer, the bank needs to approve it.
When you do increase your offer to asking price or above, you'll have the protection of the mortgage lender to confirm the value of the property. Once you have a mortgage in principle the lender values the property to assess whether it is suitable security for your mortgage loan. It doesn't confirm the current market value, it just confirms that it is a reasonable enough security to pay off your mortgage should the lender need to repossess.

If your offer is too high and the mortgage lender's valuer does not agree with the valuation for security of the mortgage, then they'll state what valuation is appropriate.

What happens if the bank undervalues the property?
Whilst this may feel devastating, in my opinion it means you've dodged a bullet. You made an offer that the mortgage lender's valuer doesn't feel reflects the value of the property and they'll

state the value they do feel is suitable security for the lender.

This has saved you paying more than what a property is worth. You can proceed with the purchase if the property is undervalued if you have enough deposit to make up the difference. This is highly unlikely and puts you at risk of negative equity from the day you purchase the property (the property value is lower than the mortgage debt plus your deposit).

It may be that there are works required, in which case the valuer will state what the property will be worth after works were completed. Where works are flagged you can get a mortgage for the lower sum and pay to get the works done. Once the work has been signed off, the lender will send the balance of the mortgage for the full value, post-works. As in the example above, you would need to make up the difference on the purchase price, and the cost of the works.

In both scenarios, you are best placed to renegotiate the purchase price to the value agreed by the mortgage lender's valuer. If the mortgage lender isn't happy to lend at the price you originally offered, then why should you proceed at that price?

CHAPTER 3

INSTRUCT A SOLICITOR

I think your choice of solicitor is so important and can have such a material bearing on your conveyancing experiences, that this chapter goes into more detail than the ones on other professionals, such as your RICS Surveyor and Mortgage Broker. The reason for this is that your solicitor will be with you from start to finish and is on the hook for making sure you know the legal risks of the property you are buying. The other professionals play a part, but the main character is your solicitor, so don't choose a bad one!

Do I have to use a solicitor?

I've had to debate at length with clients who call the office and ask, *"why do I need a solicitor"* and *"it's just form filling, I can do that, why waste the money"*. My answer, *"Good luck with that!"* and I wish them well in their doomed cause to handle a DIY conveyance, knowing full well that they'll have to use a solicitor to handle the process for them at some point, as there are a number of points in the transaction which, legally, only a solicitor can perform.

To put this quote into context, it is like saying to a Dentist who is about to conduct a root canal, *"why do I need a dentist"* and *"it's just a little tooth I can pull out with string and a door slam"*. I wouldn't do this, because I don't know the complexities around removing a tooth, how to do it painlessly or how to handle the risks along the way. Instructing a conveyancing solicitor is the same, and a good one can save you thousands in buying an overpriced property or by fixing a defective title. I'll explain more on this in *Chapter 7 – Contracts and enquiries.*

Although I've flagged their experience and knowledge as one reason you need a solicitor, there are other reasons why you must have a solicitor or licenced conveyancer to handle your conveyancing:

- ✓ Most high street lenders will only lend to you with a solicitor in place, to ensure that their interests are protected and to register their charge at the Land Registry.

- ✓ Mortgage lenders have a select panel of which specific firms of solicitors they will agree to work with.

- ✓ Solicitors should file your SDLT form online and pay your duty on time by bank transfer.

- ✓ Solicitors should register your property using the Land Registry online portal (although this can't be done if it's a new build – new builds can't be registered online, the fee is higher!).

- ✓ Solicitors can draft the deeds you may require to complete your purchase, such as a deed of covenant or a deed of trust, something that you can't do unless you are a law firm.

- ✓ A solicitor can give an undertaking, and an individual can't (an undertaking is a legal promise to do/not to do something and there are very serious legal repercussions if they don't do it).

- ✓ Most importantly, the seller's solicitor won't send sale proceeds to any account that isn't a client account, operated by a law firm.

What type of law firm do I choose?

There are two main types of regulated law firms who can act for you in the purchase of your property:

- ✓ A law firm regulated by the Solicitors Regulation Authority (SRA) which is the regulatory arm of the Law Society. You should check to see if your law firm is registered with the Law Society[17] and they should also have the SRA logo with today's date in the footer of their website.

- ✓ A conveyancing firm regulated by the Council for Licenced Conveyancers (CLC).

Throughout the book if I talk about a Solicitor, this means whoever you have chosen to act on your behalf as your legal representative.

Should I use a solicitor or a conveyancer – what's the difference?

This is one of the most common questions when searching for someone to handle the legal work on your purchase. I will start with each type of qualification they can have, and explain why it doesn't mean you get a better service:

- **Solicitor**. Depending on the type of firm you choose, a solicitor will have studied from 5 to 7 years (either a Law Degree, or another Degree followed by a conversion course, followed by the Legal Practice Course (now called SQE), had 2 years in training (known as a trainee solicitor) and then qualified as a solicitor. You can check how many years qualified the solicitor is online[18].

---

[17] https://solicitors.lawsociety.org.uk/?Pro=True
[18] https://solicitors.lawsociety.org.uk/?Pro=True

- **Licenced Conveyancer**. Trained under the regulator the Council for Licenced Conveyancers (CLC).

- **ILEX**. Trained under the Institute of Legal Executives.

The qualification isn't normally an issue as the firm who employs your conveyancer will have professional indemnity insurance and regulatory obligations for the delivery of the legal advice.

They're a bunch of phone dodgers.

After working with all types of qualified conveyancers over 20 years I can safely say this:

> *"Years' experience doesn't mean they'll pick up the phone or answer emails".*

I've seen, first-hand, solicitors, licenced conveyancers, FILEX and even conveyancers in training look at their phone, recognise the number calling in and then put their phone on Do Not Disturb (DND) because they don't want to talk to that client. Shocking. In the conveyancing world it is way too common to ignore or delay responding to clients. You only need to look at the bad reviews that some law firms receive online, to see how upsetting it can be to their clients.

Sadly, there are some lawyers out there who love the work but don't like the client interaction and would rather dodge the call than take it, only to have to tell you (probably not for the first time), that they don't have what they need from the seller, or they still haven't gotten round to what they need to do next. I cover this in more detail in *Chapter 7 – What are reasonable times to wait for stuff to get done?* and *What is the most efficient way to get an update?*

Having your calls dodged and feeling kept in the dark on something as important and personal as the purchase of your own home, may well drive you into a murderous rage. This is the main cause for the bad reputation legal professionals have in the conveyancing sector. What the conveyancer fails to see is that by ignoring your call, they are increasing the number of inbound calls by 300% because what happens next:

1) You call the estate agent because they'll pick up the phone to you and then you moan to them about not being able to get hold of their solicitor. The estate agent might have referred the seller to use this solicitor themselves...

2) You then call your mortgage broker to see if they can help.

3) What then happens is the estate agent, mortgage broker and you, all call the solicitor to get an update.

4) The 3 calls are followed by 3 emails from the estate agent, mortgage broker and yourself.

This is a complete waste of everyone's time, caused by one solicitor who didn't pick up the phone. And I must add it isn't just solicitors; this practice runs throughout the conveyancing sector. It was one of the key reasons we adopt a 3-ring policy at SAM Conveyancing, and if a single call is missed, we call you back.

Call **0333 344 3234** from 9.30am to 5pm and try for yourself. You may even find I grab the phone because the ethos in my company (which starts right at CEO level), is that **communication is key**.

More complex, more qualifications

To answer whether you need to use a solicitor, conveyancer, or any of the others from the list, you need to first find out if they have the experience and knowledge to handle some of the more bespoke transactions which first-time buyers have. Not all conveyancers can handle all types of purchases; especially new build, shared ownership, and leasehold or share of freehold.

More experience, higher fees

The more years your solicitor has under their belt, will mean the more you'll pay for their services. You'll struggle to get a low fixed fee as they'll often charge a higher fee by the hour, starting from £250 plus VAT an hour.

So, who should I choose?

In my opinion you can find a highly communicative, knowledgeable, and competitively priced trainee who you'll be thrilled with. It comes down to the individual you're working with.

How do I choose the best conveyancing solicitor?

Prior to the nineties, your conveyancing would be handled by one of the following:

- **Family solicitor.** They'd be a trusted legal advisor who would manage all the family's affairs, handling the legal work for your parents for a wide variety of services, from their first purchase to the probate of their death. The solicitor would be local because you would need to visit their office, to have an in-person meeting to pass "Know Your Client" (KYC) and to discuss any issues they had found with the property.

  You would not have even blinked an eye to pay an hourly rate of £100 to £200 per hour, with the end bill being £2,000 upward for this service. There wasn't a fixed fee and if the purchase aborted, you'd still pay for the time on the clock.

- **Estate Agent Referral.** The selling agent will work closely with their local solicitor and have a referral arrangement with them. The solicitor would pay the agent a referral fee of £100 to £500 and/or have a big budget to take the estate agent out to as many 'wine and dine' events as possible.

  You end up paying higher legal fees as the solicitor builds in the cost of the referral fee to the estate agent. This is still the practice today.

The issue I have with working with the estate agent's referred solicitor is that the agent has been employed by the seller to sell the property for the highest price possible, as quickly as possible and, (even though they won't say this) with as few questions as possible. So why on Earth would you as the buyer even entertain working with a solicitor they refer?

The solicitor will tell you that they are impartial, and I think that they believe that. In practise though, the solicitor may be torn between acting in their client's best interest (that's you), vs the estate agent's best interest (remember the agent is acting for the seller), in order to maintain the commercial arrangement where they benefit from, say, 50 client referrals a month through this local agent.

Times have changed since the internet came along and now you have new parties at the table looking to attract your business:

1. **Online law firms**. These are the tech savvy local law firms that chose to market their services online. I often get asked, "are you just online?" and the answer is simple: we're on a high street like yours, but we market online.

2. **Online comparison sites**. These comparison sites dominate the top search terms in Google and their goal is to provide you with 10 estimates, all too low and too good to be true.

3. **Hybrid Concierge Conveyancing.** In a hybrid model a website generates leads, introduces the client to the solicitor, and case manages the process, like *SAM Conveyancing*. You get a specialist solicitor and someone to manage the service delivery and communication.

When do I need to instruct a solicitor?

You need a solicitor from the point your offer is accepted by the seller, because the estate agents need to issue the sales memorandum to both solicitors before draft contracts can be issued and the conveyancing process can get underway.

As I explained in *Chapter 2 - Summary of what you need to make a Winning Offer* your offer will be taken more seriously by the seller and estate agent if you have already instructed a solicitor. It means you are serious about buying the property and have most likely sent your ID and proof of funds evidence to your solicitor as well as paid them your instruction deposit, which gives you a head start over another buyer who has not yet instructed. For this reason, if you are ready to make an offer, you should have your solicitor instructed and on standby.

There is no downside to doing this, especially if you have a solicitor who works on a No Sale No Fee guarantee, or who won't charge you until you get an offer accepted. The only downside is if you weren't really interested in that specific property and are likely to either pull out all together or wait to find another property.

What are the costs of buying a house?

On your hunt to find a solicitor you'll be met with a variety of costs. The way that these are laid out can make the mind boggle. The actual costs shouldn't vary, except for the price your solicitor charges for their services.

Here are the costs you should expect to pay:

- **Legal Fee**. This is what your solicitor is charging you for their legal services. Prices range from £400 up to, and beyond, £2,000. Whilst the cheaper price seems appealing, it often comes with a huge number of add-ons, just like budget airlines.

To avoid getting an unexpected bill at the end, make sure to get a Fixed Fee Quote that includes all the legal fees for a standard transaction. Additional legal fees should only be added on for work that falls outside of a standard transaction. The extra fees to watch out for are: SDLT filing fee, bank transfer fee, mortgage fee, leasehold fee, and online access fee – all of which are standard and should be included in your fixed fee.

A freehold is cheaper than a leasehold because there is less work. A leasehold should be cheaper than buying through an affordable housing scheme for the same reason.

- **Stamp Duty Land Tax (SDLT).** You pay tax on any transfer of land where the consideration (price paid) is above a certain limit. There is often a relief for first time buyers to help them on the property ladder. You can use this online calculator[19] to see what the stamp duty is on your purchase.

- **Land Registration Fee.** This is the cost for updating the Land Registry with your name. The cost depends on the property value. You can check the current fee online[20].

- **Conveyancing Searches.** The main 4 are the Local Authority Search, Water and Drainage Search, Environmental Search and Chancel Search. The cost is often bundled together from £265. If you are paying more than this,

---

[19] https://www.samconveyancing.co.uk/stamp-duty-calculator
[20] https://www.samconveyancing.co.uk/news/conveyancing/land-registry-registration-fees-244#ONE

you can buy your own[21].

- **Online ID Check.** This is the cost for verifying your ID. Costs range from £8 to £50 per buyer and for anyone providing any money toward the purchase.

- **Lawyer Checker.** This disbursement is paid to validate the bank account details for the seller's solicitor, to avoid fraud by money being sent to an incorrect bank account. It costs between £15 and £30.

- **Land Registry Priority (OS1).** Costs £3. Paid prior to exchange, to protect the legal title (your property) from any unauthorised changes being made.

- **Land Registry Bankruptcy Search.** Costs £2 per buyer and is paid prior to exchange, to ensure the buyers haven't had a bankruptcy application made against them.

You'll pay for the Conveyancing Searches and part of your solicitor's legal fees on instruction of the purchase. The rest of the costs are paid the day before you complete. We cover this in more detail in *Chapter 9 - What does a completion statement look like?*

Here are some extra costs that you may have to pay if you're buying a leasehold:

- **Apportionments.** There'll be ground rent and service charge apportionments that you'll need to reimburse the seller for because they've been paid already, or there'll be an allowance because they haven't yet been paid. In essence you're making sure you only pay for the charges

---

[21] https://www.samconveyancing.co.uk/news/conveyancing/property-searches-which-searches-do-you-need-131#SEARCHES

relevant from the date that you take ownership of the property.

- **Deed of Covenant.** This is a legal document which states that the leaseholder agrees to undertake an obligation, or series of obligations, laid out by the freeholder (or landlord). The Deed is essentially the document that states the covenants (or promises) that should be adhered to when a new leasehold property owner takes control. You'll need to pay the freeholder's solicitor for drafting the deed. Costs range from £240 to £600. You'll also need to pay your solicitor for reviewing and executing with it, at a cost of around £240.

Here are some extra costs that you may have to pay if you're buying a new build:

- **Engrossment Fee.** The seller's solicitor charges the buyer an engrossment fee for producing the legal document that will transfer ownership from the seller to the buyer. Costs range from £80 to £360. You'll also need to pay your solicitor for reviewing and executing it, £120.

What happens after I instruct a solicitor?
The first few days after you instruct your solicitor are very busy. Here's what needs to happen:

- ✓ **Send details to your estate agent**. The estate agent needs to issue the Sales Memorandum which includes yours and the buyer's solicitor's details. If you delay in providing your solicitor's details, then the seller's solicitor is unable to issue contracts and the process will stall.

- ✓ **Instruction Documents**. Sign and return your solicitor's Letter of Instruction. Your solicitor is unable to conduct any work on your behalf until they've received this. If there is a delay in sending back your signed instruction letter, the process will once again stall.

✓ **Proof of ID**. You provide your photo ID (passport or driving licence) and proof of address (bank statement or utility bill from last 3 months) to your solicitor.

✓ **Proof of Funds**. Evidence of how you have accumulated the money you are using to buy the property. We cover this in the next section.

Some solicitors have online or mobile Apps you can use to instruct them and provide your ID, though some solicitors still prefer email, and some post. If the latter, be prepared for your solicitor's processes to be slower than others that use tech to speed up the conveyancing process.

How to prove source of funds

"I'm not a criminal, so why so many questions?"

The UK is #2 on the list of global money laundering hotspots, new research from Credas[22] has found. The study found that an estimated £88 billion is laundered every year in the UK.

Your solicitor has a legal obligation to check, to their satisfaction, that the money you are using to fund your purchase has come from a legitimate source and not from illegal activity. This isn't your solicitor being awkward, it is legally required by the Money Laundering, Terrorist Financing and Transfer of Funds (Information on the Payer) Regulations 2017 (and its amendments)

---

[22] https://www.fstech.co.uk/fst/UK_Comes_Second_Place_For_Global_Money_Laundering.php?mc_cid=4621fe70b5&mc_eid=55189edf5d

(the MLR) and Proceeds of Crime Act 2002 (POCA 2002). There are serious consequences for your solicitor and the Law Firm if they fail to comply with this legislation.

For most first-time buyers, proving the source of your funds is a simple process, as it'll most likely be showing your monthly savings for your deposit from your salary, and potentially a gift from mum and dad. Here are the different sources of income and the evidence required to prove where it came from.

Savings from income	Copies of your last 6-12 months' pay slips from your employer, and 3 months bank statements
Multiple savings accounts	Copies of your last 6-12 months' bank statements.
ISA	Copy of your latest ISA statement showing the money transferring to your account and Copies of 6-12 months' bank statements.
LISA	Completed LISA declaration.
Inheritance	Copy of the letter from the executor, confirming the amount paid to you as a beneficiary to the estate and Copies of 6-12 months' bank statements.
Sale of Shares	Copy of the share certificate confirming the sale and Copies of 6-12 months' bank statements.
Dividends	Copy of the confirmation of dividend pay-out and Copies of 6-12 months' bank statements.

Cash	You cannot use cash to buy a property. Whether it is cash in your hand or cash you have paid into your bank account. If the source is from cash, then you cannot use it.
Crypto	You cannot use cryptocurrency to buy a property. If you cash in crypto into your bank account, then you'll not be able to use those funds to buy your property.

The above is typical of what you might be asked to provide. Your own solicitor may require more/less evidence to prove the source of your funds. The reason for this is that every solicitor has their own Money Laundering Policy. Some take different views on the risk of different sources and as such will request less or more information. Some solicitors may request the documents scanned into PDF format, or copied or printed to hard copy, in the post.

I'm not giving you that "Personal Information".

You're correct to flag that the financial statements and evidence from third parties is personal information (data), which is why your solicitor must protect this data under their General Data Protection Regulations (GDPR) policy.

By law, your solicitor cannot share your personal data with anyone, unless requested to do so under a criminal investigation. If this is a concern, then you'll have a problem, as all law firms are governed by the Data Protection Laws. Breaching your personal data rights is a serious matter and your solicitor is legally and professionally prohibited from doing so.

Reluctance to share personal information may present an issue for you, as it raises red flags to your solicitor who may suspect you have something to hide.

The same will happen with proving the source of your funds; the more obstructive you are, the more red flags are raised, and the greater the chance your solicitor will refuse to receive the funds you want to use. In the end you'll be left with no option but to find a new solicitor – and then face the same questions.

If you've nothing to hide, just provide the solicitor with the information they request, in the format they ask for it, and in a timely fashion.

What evidence do you need for a gift?

Whether you have already received the gift, or you are going to receive it before exchange, you'll need the gift giver to prove the source of *their* funds. You will also need to declare this gift to your mortgage lender, which I cover in *Chapter 4 – Is a gift ok from family and friends?*

What if the money originates from outside England and Wales?

When you use money from outside of England and Wales, whether the funds are currently in your bank account or not, the account holder must provide:

- ✓ **Notarised Passport.** If the account holder is a non-UK resident, they need to take their passport to a local solicitor or notary in the country they reside in. The passport is photocopied and certified by the solicitor or notary. If the account holder owns a UK passport and they are a UK resident, they can send a scan of their passport along with their National Insurance number and the solicitor will complete an Online ID check.

- ✓ **Proof of address.** Proof of address can be a copy of a utility bill or bank statement, from within the last 3 months. The name and address must match the bank statement where the funds are being sent from. This document does not need to be translated.

✓ **Proof of the source of funds**. You need to provide evidence of how the money was accrued (see pg. 61 & 62) and 6-12 months bank statements. All non-English evidence needs to be translated into English by a third party and, in addition, the monetary figures on bank statements must be converted into sterling (GBP). You can use the current exchange rate as at today. It doesn't need to be accurate as of a future date as you are only evidencing what money is being paid into and paid out of the bank account and its value in sterling. You cannot translate your own documents. (Further evidence maybe requested, if required, to meet with the solicitor's Money Laundering Procedures).

Which countries can a solicitor not receive money from?

Part of the new Money Laundering Regulations requires solicitors to decline instructions from clients or a beneficial owner who is resident in, or has a substantial connection to, a high-risk country, or who possesses relevant assets in a high-risk country.

You cannot receive money from any country listed on the Law Society's High-risk third countries for AML purposes[23]. If you are planning on using funds from a high-risk country, then your solicitor cannot act on your behalf, and neither should anyone else.

---

[23] The Law Society's High Risk Countries - https://www.lawsociety.org.uk/topics/anti-money-laundering/high-risk-third-countries-for-aml-purposes

CHAPTER 4

HOW ARE YOU FINANCING THE PURCHASE?

Overview of the mortgage process

I think this is one of the biggest hurdles for first-time buyers, as it is a real deal breaker for you. If you can't get a mortgage, then you can't buy your first home. It is a process where I've found the help of a mortgage broker to be invaluable. Alternatively, you may choose to apply directly with a bank or building society of your own choice.

Whether you use a broker or apply direct, the process to get a mortgage offer is the same:

1) **Mortgage illustration** – based on limited information you'll be informed of what your likely mortgage value could be. I suggest you get one of these as soon as possible, as I flagged earlier, it'll help you get your offer accepted and prove you're a serious buyer.

2) **Mortgage in Principle** – this is where you make a formal mortgage application and your lender:
   a) Confirms your ID,
   b) Undertakes credit checks,
   c) Reviews evidence of deposit,
   d) Reviews your income.

3) **Mortgage valuation** – the lender instructs a RICS surveyor to value the property.

4) **Mortgage offer** – you get the lender's final agreement to lend to you. This can only be pulled in very few circumstances.

Is a gift ok from family and friends?

Most mortgage lenders allow you to receive a gift as part of your deposit if it is from your legal parents, subject to proof of funds checks and a gift declaration, which we cover in *Chapter 4 – What evidence do you need for a gift*?

Fewer lenders allow gifts from siblings and other family members and even fewer from friends. The reason is that the legal default presumes that any money from mum and dad is a gift and any money from siblings and friends is a loan. I.e., they'll want the money back.

You should speak to your mortgage broker and let them know where your gift is coming from, they'll know which lenders will agree to the gift.

Don't assume that money is yours once it is in your bank account and won't still count as a gift. The source of funds will flag the money came from someone else and the gift will be referred to the lender by your solicitor. This wastes time at the very late stages of the conveyancing process. You will only have yourself to blame if the mortgage offer is pulled and you have to scrabble around to find a new lender who will agree to the gift source and then apply for a new mortgage with them.

How to get a mortgage

The mortgage application process is the same for all mortgage lenders and follows this simple checking process:

- Are you good with money?
- Have you got a big enough deposit and where does it come from?
- How much do you earn each year?
- Can you afford the mortgage?

And it isn't like a Meatloaf song where "2 out of 3 ain't bad". With a mortgage application, you need to pass all the above to be sure to get a mortgage.

Although, with this said, there are some lenders who support higher risk applications. Be careful, because the higher the risk, the higher your interest rate will be. To see this in practice, look at the interest rates for a fixed rate deal for a first-time buyer with a 10% deposit versus one with a 40% deposit. The latter is less risk to the lender, and as such will benefit from a cheaper interest rate.

You should also factor in, *"if the interest rate rises, will you still be able to afford the monthly payments when you come to re-mortgage the property in 1, 2 or 5-years' time?"* My advice is, don't over stretch yourself at the outset, as this could have serious consequences a few years down the line. More on this later.

How do I prove my income for the mortgage multiples?
The amount of money you are offered in a mortgage relies upon the amount of money you earn and how much you spend. Depending on your mortgage term and your age you'll be offered somewhere between 4 to 5 times your gross income for the year.

For example:
- You are a 25-year-old with a gross salary of £30,000 where your employer handles your PAYE. You are looking for a 35-year mortgage.
- You are offered a 4.5 times salary mortgage.
- This equates to a mortgage of £135,000.
- Add this to your deposit of 10% or more. That is the total

amount you can afford to buy a property for. (£148,500 +)

You may have various additional types of income and mortgage lenders can take into consideration other employment income such as commission or an annual bonus.

> ➤ **Gross Basic Salary**. This is what you are contracted to receive from your employer through PAYE. All lenders will be happy with you evidencing what this is through your last 6 months' payslips.
> ➤ **Commission.** This is variable based on what you achieve each month, and most mortgage lenders take this into account on an average basis over 6-12 months. You can prove this income through your last 6 months payslips.
> ➤ **Bonus.** Large, one-off bonuses can be taken into consideration, but much like commission the bonus for the last 1-3 years will be requested. You can prove this income through the payslips from when you received the bonus.

What do I do if I'm Self-Employed?

Mortgage lenders will need to see your end of year self-assessment SA302 (confirmation of income and tax paid) for the last 3 to 6 years. If you've had one bumper year, but the previous 3 weren't so great, then the mortgage lender will take this into account.

What do I do if I own my company?

At present, dividends attract a lower tax rate than PAYE income, so company owners pay themselves a smaller income and the balance via dividends (distribution from profits after corporation tax known as "Profit After Tax (PAT)"). The mortgage lender will want to see company accounts for the past 3-6 years to calculate the PAT trend. Much like a self-employed application, having one amazing year doesn't always mean they'll use that figure for the mortgage multiples.

How do I prove my affordability?

Back in the early 2000s if you had a good salary and a 10% deposit then mortgage lenders would class you as "self-certifying" your mortgage and pay little to no interest in your affordability. This was great because you had no worry of not getting a mortgage, so long as you could stump up the 10% deposit.

Following the financial crash in 2008 mortgage lending criteria became tougher and in 2016 measures were introduced that meant mortgage lenders had to be more responsible when lending mortgages. This was called the Mortgage Market Review[24] .

The review meant that mortgage lenders needed to look beyond the deposit and salary of the applicant; they needed to inspect their affordability as well. Does the applicant have enough spare income to increase their payments if interest rates go up? Often known as disposable income, this is the sum of money you have spare after paying all the essential monthly outgoings.

Whilst some mortgage applicants had large salaries, what the new affordability measures flagged was whether that salary was equally being consumed by huge monthly commitments such as:

- Hire purchases
- Gym memberships
- Subscriptions
- Pay-day loans
- Online betting

If you have too much of a drain on your monthly finances then

---

[24] Financial Services Authority Mortgage Market Review: Responsible Lending - https://www.fca.org.uk/publication/consultation/fsa-cp10-16.pdf

even if you have a large deposit and sizeable salary, you could be turned down based on the other financial commitments you have each month, which could affect your ability to pay your mortgage repayments if they increase due to interest rates increasing. Essentially, the lender will recognise that your income is already spent.

To make your affordability stronger you should trim down on any excess subscriptions, memberships and expenses in the 6 months running up to a mortgage application. By doing this you are showing that you have strong disposable income.

An absolute red warning is if you have spent a lot of money with online gambling sites. A mortgage lender sees gambling as an unstable expense, meaning that month to month you may not be able to afford your repayments.

Another no-no are payday loans. If you use pay day loans, you are advertising to a mortgage lender that you have previously been unable to afford your outgoings. Once again this is telling your mortgage lender that there is a risk you won't manage your finances and could end up without the money to pay all your monthly mortgage repayments.

What are the different types of mortgage product?

Fixed Rate	You fix the interest rate of your mortgage for 2, 3, 5 or sometimes 10 years. At the end of your fixed term, the interest reverts to the mortgage lender's standard variable rate. This goes up with, and is normally higher than, the Bank of England base rate.
Tracker	Tracker mortgages have a variable interest rate that tracks the Bank of England base rate plus a set

percentage.

For example, the base rate reached 4% at the beginning of 2023. So, if your tracker is 'base rate plus 3%', you'd pay a rate of 7%.

The tracker has a fixed deal period, commonly 2 years, after which it goes onto the lender's standard variable rate.

Discount mortgages	Discount mortgages have a variable interest rate based on the lender's standard variable rate (SVR) minus a fixed margin. For example, if your lender's SVR is 5% and your Discount Mortgage charges the SVR minus 2%, you'll pay a rate of 3%.

You need a good credit score.

Your credit score is an online assessment of who you are, how you handle paying monthly bills and how much credit you have available to you. Mortgage lenders look at this like it is your financial CV. Have you missed any loan payments? How many credit cards do you have? Do you move around a lot?

You are a low risk if you have low credit available, pay your monthly bills on time, you have stayed in one location for a long time and have all your addresses updated. You are higher risk if any of these aren't correctly managed.

You can check your credit score on a wide variety of platforms for free. When getting a mortgage, I would suggest using the paid for service from Equifax or Experian (I use the latter) in the run up to getting a mortgage, so you can fix any issues you may find. Your mortgage lender uses the report from either of these two sites, so knowing what they will see and fixing issues before they see it, will mean a higher chance of getting your mortgage approved.

How do I improve my credit score?

Here are a few ways to make your credit score the best it can be:

✓ *Get a credit card, spend, and pay it off.*
Yes, I'm telling you to get a credit card and spend it. I'm also saying pay it off in full every month no matter what. It is important to show your mortgage lender that you handle your credit responsibly and never miss a payment.

This process works even if you only spend £5 on your credit card and then set it up to pay off in full by direct debit on the day after you get paid your salary.

✓ *Update all your personal details.*
This is so simple to do but it is a huge red flag for a mortgage lender if they see that you have multiple addresses linked to you – why? Because they want to know where you live to enforce any debt you owe them.

To fix this, download your credit report, contact every company on there and update your current home address.

✓ *Trim down available credit*
Even if you have £20,000 limit on your credit card and you've used next to none of it, you need to close that card down or reduce the limit. Your mortgage lender will look at the available limit of all your credit cards and will flag it as a risk that you could, if you wanted to, go on a spending spree the day after completion and rack up debt to the sum limit of all your lines of credit.

Reduce this risk by closing credit and store cards you don't use and keep the limit of available credit to circa £2,000.

✓ *Stop moving around.*
In the run up to your mortgage application you should try and stay put for 3 to 6 months. Make sure all your addresses are updated as above.

✓ *Don't live with people who have a bad credit score.*
Your credit rating could be adversely affected if you live with someone with a bad credit rating. For example, if your partner has been made bankrupt while registered at your address.

Now you know how to make your credit score the best it can be, you need to prove that you are paid enough from your employer and that the source of your funds is legit!

Show me the MONEY!!!

You've got a 10% deposit and earn a fat salary, why do they need to know what you spend your money on as well? Well, it goes back to the Financial Crash in September 2007 and the effects that caused the mortgage application process to grow up and ask more questions.

For anyone who doesn't know what the Financial Crash was, you'll find cleverer people than I, who can explain it in a much better way. I'd summarise the crash in one sentence:

"Banks lent to people who couldn't afford the mortgage, that was secured on properties that were overpriced, and then the banks sold the mortgage debts to other banks, branded as low risk – and then borrowers couldn't afford their mortgage repayments".

It was known as sub-prime lending and when people stopped paying their mortgages and the repossessions started, those banks that had bought those 'low risk' debts took huge losses. The largest scalp was Lehman Brothers and according to Wikipedia it states:

"On September 15, 2008, Lehman Brothers filed for Chapter 11 bankruptcy protection following the exodus of most of its clients, drastic declines in its stock price, and the devaluation of assets by credit rating agencies. The collapse was largely due to Lehman's involvement in the subprime mortgage crisis and its exposure to less liquid assets. Lehman's bankruptcy filing was the largest in US history and is thought to have played a major role in the unfolding of the financial crisis of 2007–2008. The market collapse also gave support to the "Too big to fail" doctrine." [25].

It wasn't just a small issue. We're not talking one hundred mortgages that had an issue, we are talking thousands of mortgages being loaned to people who should never have been loaned the money.

The problem is easy to see now; if you lend money to someone who can't afford it, on a property that isn't worth what they paid, then if the borrower stops paying the mortgage, the bank will need to sell quickly. It's sold for under what was paid, and often under the actual debt value leaving the balance unpaid. That debt is still something the homeowner is liable for, so they are left with no home and outstanding debt.

The film The Big Short[26] with Christian Bale is a good one to watch to get more of an insight into the Financial Crash. It is a true story, and his character predicted the crash and profited from betting against the market.

What made this crash stand out, was how widespread

---

[25] https://en.wikipedia.org/wiki/Lehman_Brothers
[26] https://www.imdb.com/title/tt1596363/

throughout the world it was felt. It really was a global crash and in England we saw most of our high street banks affected. Two of the most notable were the Royal Bank of Scotland and Northern Rock.

The Royal Bank of Scotland (RBS) was one of the banks bailed out at the height of the financial crisis in 2008, it received public funds to the effect of £45.5bn. In 2019, RBS paid a total dividend of £2.7bn to shareholders, of which £1.7bn was returned to the UK taxpayer – *"that's you and me!!!"*

Northern Rock on the other hand was in far too bad a financial position to be bailed out by the Government. Their balance sheet was dire as it was full of assets (properties) valued at more than they were worth. The writing was on the wall, anyone with a bank account queued up outside the bank to draw out their money. North Rock went under and to be honest I'm not surprised.

For years Northern Rock was one of the leading first-time buyer mortgage lenders and offered 100% to 125% mortgage products. Yup, that's right, you could buy a house with no deposit and even get the bank to pay you 25% over what it was worth. Sounds nuts, and it was nuts, but for years house prices had been going up and up and up, so why not get even more people on the housing market to then benefit from this assumed increase in the future.

I saw this, first hand, when in 2001, at the age of 21, I was able to join the housing market with a Northern Rock 10% deposit and 'self-certified' 90% mortgage, with no affordability checks. I later heard that in 2006, before I met my wife, she got a 125% Northern Rock mortgage and used the extra 25% to pay off credit cards (probably buying shoes). Credit (mortgages, loans, and credit cards) was so easy to get back then - why wouldn't you take it if it was on offer? As my wife used to say back then, *"it's like free money"*. Little did she know that less than 2 years later, Northern Rock would be no more.

Why do you need to know this? Well, it is because of this irresponsible lender that mortgage lenders now need to investigate your affordability in more detail. They need to know where your deposit is coming from, what your salary is and is likely to be, what you spend your money on, and whether you can afford to absorb the increase in mortgage repayments, if interest rates go up.

Why do I have to prove I can afford the mortgage?

During the mortgage application process, you'll need to provide 6 to 12 months' bank statements, to prove what you spend your money on and to ensure that you can afford your mortgage repayments with a buffer in case the banks increase the mortgage interest.

"But I'm on a fixed rate deal for 5 years, so what's the issue?"

The fixed rate only lasts for so long and after it expires you go onto the bank's standard variable rate (SVR), which is higher than the Bank of England base rate. Your mortgage lasts for many more years than your fixed term, and your mortgage lender needs to know that if you are unable to secure a new fixed rate deal when your fixed term ends, that you will be able to afford the mortgage once it reverts to the Standard Variable Rate.

There are millions of homeowners who are living in a property they can't afford, which means they are spiralling into more and more debt. Mortgage lenders don't want to risk you being unable to pay your mortgage repayments, so they will test your finances to see if you can afford the mortgage, right up to 6-9% interest rates[27]. For more on the risks, jump to *Chapter 10 - What happens if I can't afford to repay my mortgage?*

Should I secure a fixed rate for 2 or 5 years?

---

[27] https://www.bbc.co.uk/news/business-63961179

This question is particularly interesting at the beginning of 2023. Interest rates are relatively high (though not nearly as high as they have been in economic crises of the past), and borrowers are having to gamble on how long it is going to take for them to return to normal. The shorter the fixed term, the greater the risk that rates will be higher when your fixed-rate period ends, and you will not be able to afford your mortgage repayments. In a worst-case-scenario, this could mean the bank repossesses your property. The longer the fixed term, the higher the risk that average rates fall below yours and you pay more than you'd otherwise have to. You also lose some flexibility.

There is comfort in having a fixed rate for 5 years because if you know you can afford it then it'll help you budget. The problem is if the Bank of England base rate goes down, then you could be stuck on a higher interest rate than current deals at the time.

As an example, in November 2021 base rate was 0.1% but by February 2023 it had risen to 4%. Knowing this, you'd be better to have secured your fixed rate mortgage for 5 years at the lower rate, instead of 2 years. The interest on mortgages will be higher come November 2023 if the base rate remains at 4%[28].

Should I secure a mortgage for 25, 30, 35 or 40 years?

This comes down to how much you can afford and, in most cases, (because you want to make the monthly mortgage payments more affordable) you'll choose a longer mortgage term. Here are the principles:

> A longer mortgage term means you pay more interest over the life of the mortgage, but your monthly mortgage repayments will be smaller.

---

[28] https://www.bbc.co.uk/news/business-63961179

➢ A shorter mortgage term means you pay less interest over the life of the mortgage, but your monthly mortgage repayments will be more.

What do you do once you get a mortgage offer?

Do a little jig! Honestly for me the three best feelings in the conveyancing process were, when I got a mortgage offer, when I exchanged and then when I got my keys. The latter two I cover later, but being accepted for a mortgage offer is such an amazing achievement.

You passed the credit score, affordability, you had a big enough deposit, and they believe you are a safe bet to offer several hundred thousand pounds to. What you now need to do is read the mortgage offer and check all the details are correct including the fixed term, interest rate, mortgage illustration and special conditions. Make sure you read the mortgage lender's terms and conditions and you understand the whole document.

You'll see that the difference between the mortgage you borrowed, versus the total amount you have to pay back over the full life of the mortgage, is huge. Often hundreds of thousands of pounds more. That's all the interest you're paying the lender in exchange for holding their money over all that time.

You mortgage may come with some conditions, and I'll list a few of these below:

✓ **Occupier Waiver Form**[29]. This is needed for anyone over 16/17 years old who, will live in the property but who aren't named on the mortgage deed. The mortgage lender wants to make sure they have no legal right to reside in the property or a claim to the beneficial interest in the property. Without this waiver, the

---

[29] https://www.samconveyancing.co.uk/news/conveyancing/occupier-consent-form-what-does-your-mortgage-lender-need-6019

occupier's interest could conflict with the lender's, in the event that they must repossess. The form requires an independent solicitor to advise the party before they sign it, and the signature needs a witness. Costs for this advice range from £180 to £300.

✓ **Gifted Deposit Certificate.** This is needed for any gifts being paid from third parties. It confirms the money is a gift and not a loan. (So that the lender won't have to fight the gift-giver over any share of the equity if they must repossess). There are some lenders who allow it to be a gift repayable on sale. They sign it, and the signature needs a witness.

✓ **Guarantor Independent Legal Advice[30].** This is needed for some mortgage products, such as a Joint Mortgage Sole Proprietor. The party who is named on the mortgage but not getting the benefit from the property will need independent legal advice as to the risks of the transaction with an independent solicitor. Costs for this advice range from £180 to £300.

How do you sign a mortgage deed?

Once your mortgage offer is issued your solicitor will either be sent a hard copy in the post/email, or they'll be able to download it from the LMS Portal. Read *Chapter 8 - What is the LMS portal for mortgage lenders?* Your solicitor gets a different version of your mortgage offer to you, with instructions on what the lender wants them to do.

You solicitor acts for you *and* the mortgage lender, so needs to satisfy any lender requirements in the mortgage offer before they can issue your Mortgage Report. The Mortgage Report explains some of the key parts of the mortgage product, however you still need to have read every line of the terms and mortgage offer carefully, before your sign the mortgage deed.

---

[30] https://www.samconveyancing.co.uk/news/conveyancing/independent-legal-advice-4849

The mortgage deed is what is used to register the mortgage charge at the Land Registry, post completion, so make sure your name, the property address and any other details are correct. The mortgage deed needs signing and witnessing. See *Chater 8 – Who can be a witness?*

By 2024, expect to see mortgage deeds signed electronically. I say 2024, but it could be 2025, 2026. No matter what, digital signing for deeds going to the Land Registry is coming – at last!

Can a mortgage offer be rescinded?

Over 100 people a month Google search to see if a mortgage lender can pull their mortgage offer. The answer is yes, they can, but normally for very good reasons, such as if you made misrepresentations during your mortgage application (you lied).

Even during COVID, mortgage lenders didn't start pulling mortgage offers for no reason. It states in most mortgage terms "We may withdraw this offer if any of the following circumstances apply and, had we been aware of the true circumstances, we would not have provided the offer to you, or we would have provided an offer of a lower amount or on different terms:"

* There is a material change to the facts and circumstances relating to your loan application;
* There has been a material change in your circumstances since you applied for the mortgage which is likely to have a material impact on your ability to afford the loan;
* Where we have instructed a conveyancer they are unable to certify the title to the property in accordance with our instructions;
* There is a change to the condition, value or title to the property or we revalue the property after the date of this offer and such change or the revaluation has a material impact on the suitability of the property as security for the loan;

- ✸ We discover that you have intentionally provided us with false, inaccurate or incomplete information as part of your application for the loan or omitted information which we have requested from you as part of your application for the loan;
- ✸ We reasonably suspect you are involved in any criminal or fraudulent activity, or you are convicted of a serious criminal offence;
- ✸ Completion of the offer does not take place by the deadline given at the beginning of this offer; or
- ✸ We are no longer permitted to lend the money to you due to our regulator removing or restricting our permission to lend.

In all the transactions I've worked on I've seen less than a handful of mortgage offers pulled and they all had a very good reason. One was an HSBC mortgage where, on the day of completion, the lender found out the money to complete was sourced from cash being laundered through this poor 18 year old's bank account. The mortgage offer was pulled, he was arrested, and the Serious Organised Crime Unit (SOCA) seized the money.

Pulling a mortgage offer is bad business for mortgage lenders because it means solicitors lose faith in the lender and can't rely on them releasing the money after they have offered it. Of all the things you need to worry about, if you didn't do anything wrong on your mortgage application, this one you can ignore and bust out your happy dance!

CHAPTER 5

ARE THERE ANY DEFECTS WITH MY PROPERTY?

What are the different types of surveys?
Primary Surveys

1) *RICS Level 1 Home Survey for newer properties.* Its scope is very limited so you may not find many surveyors who offer this.

2) *RICS Level 2 Home Survey (known as the Homebuyer Report)* for a wide variety of properties such as any leasehold flat (including conversions), and standard construction houses, with or without extensions, dating back to 1920/30. The scope of work is wider than for Level 1, but not as detailed as a Level 3 Home Survey.

3) *RICS Level 3 Home Survey (known as the Building Survey or Full Structural Survey)* is for any type of property that more than 100 years old, is not a flat, is unique in build, or is larger, requiring more time to be spent in the property.

4) *Snagging Survey for new builds.* It'll flag build quality issues you can ask the developer to make good before/after you move in. It can be provided by anyone qualified to identify snags.

Additional Surveys

1) *Structural Engineer's Report* for the removal of a load bearing wall or chimney breast, or subsidence reports. A structural engineer provides this service, normally on the back of an issue that is found within a Home Survey or the mortgage valuation. If the latter, you can't proceed with the purchase until your lender is satisfied that the issue does not undervalue the property.

2) *Damp and Timber Report* will confirm the condition of the wood timber in the property and damp readings. Much like above, you normally get this specialist report if the issue has first been noted in a Home Survey.

3) *Asbestos Survey* for confirming whether materials used to build the property contain asbestos. Samples are taken by a specialist surveyor and sent to a lab for testing.

There are several surveys that are required after a defect is found in a primary survey. I'm often asked, *"why can't I jump straight to the additional survey?"* The answer is that you don't know you need an Additional Survey until you are on notice from the seller or from a surveyor that there is an issue; why waste money on additional surveys you may not need?

A RICS surveyor is like a GP. They'll inspect all visible and accessible areas of the property and grounds, note the condition and flag issues as they go. It is a full once-over of the property.

Much like a GP, when they suspect a defect, such as asbestos or subsidence/movement, they'll refer you to a specialist for prognosis. This may come back negative, but if the suspicion is confirmed then you'll be able to assess whether you proceed with your original offer or look to renegotiate or pull out of the purchase all together.

Why do I need to survey the property?

Getting an independent RICS surveyor isn't a mandatory part of the conveyancing process, and some buyers choose to skip it to save money. With the cost ranging from £499 upward, the saving is material. In the long run, it may cost you even more to skip the survey, as when buying a property in England and Wales, the property is:

"Sold as seen – Buyer Beware!"

This means that if you didn't spot it, and the seller didn't lie about it in their Property Information Forms, then you are liable for the cost of fixing it.

Insider tip: Surveyors charge more for a Level 3 Home Survey than a Level 2 Home Survey and the price goes up the more expensive, large, or unique the property.

How much do property defects cost to fix?

These are rough guides but are some of the most common issues that can be raised as a suspicion:

Defect	Problem with electrics or boiler
Description	A RICS surveyor doesn't test the utilities and can only comment on visible age and condition.
	Properties built before 2000 are going to have ageing boilers and fuse boards so expect your surveyor to flag this. Does this mean they don't work? No, it does mean they are getting old and will likely need replacing.
Cost	£300 Electrical survey. £2,000+ for a rewire and new fuse board.

£300 Boiler inspection.
£1,500+ for a new boiler.

Defect	**Drains**
Description	A RICS surveyor will, where accessible, lift manhole covers to check the drains. Where these are blocked, you may need to employ a drain specialist to attend and inspect what the blockage is and who is responsible for this (see Water and Drainage Search).
Cost	£240 For a drainage survey. £100 upward depending on responsibility for maintaining the drains.

Defect	**Removal of a load bearing wall**
Description	A RICS surveyor will flag if they note a load bearing wall has been removed. This should be registered at Building Control and noted in your Local Authority Search. If the work wasn't registered then you'll need a structural engineer to inspect the property to confirm if the wall was loadbearing, and if so, whether the structure was appropriately reinforced (requires intrusive inspection).
Cost	£599+ for a Structural Engineer's Report. £4,000+ for reinforcing and getting building control sign off.

Defect	**Damp**
Description	A selection of rooms is tested for high moisture levels using a moisture meter and any high readings will be noted in the report. You'll need a Damp Surveyor to inspect the property to confirm the cause and potential costs for making good.
Cost	£499+ for a Damp Survey. £10,000+ for damp proofing.

Defect	**Movement**
Description	Also known as subsidence, a surveyor will raise any cause for concern on this. It doesn't always mean you have subsidence, but that there are signs which merit further investigation. A structural engineer will need to attend the property and first visually inspect, then if required carry out an intrusive inspection of the footings.
Cost	£599+ for non-intrusive review. £3,000+ for intrusive review. £40,00+ for underpinning.

Defect	**Infestation**
Description	Those pesky rats, mice, wood worm, could all

	impact the property.
Cost	£300+

Defect	**Japanese Knotweed**
Description	The surveyor will flag if they see signs of Japanese Knotweed in the garden. This weed can burrow into your foundations and cause movement/subsidence. It is incredibly invasive and fast growing. It is often found near railway lines. A Japanese Knotweed specialist is needed to confirm the issue and put together a treatment plan to remove it.
Cost	£400+ for a Japanese Knotweed Survey. £3,000+ for a Treatment Plan.

+ means get a quote as actual costs vary significantly, do not rely on my estimate.

The reports cover more than just the above, such as chimney breasts, drains, roofs, lofts/extension, insulation. If you're not sure what type of survey to get on your property, call the survey team at SAM Conveyancing at your local rate, on 0333 344 3234. We'll help you choose the correct level for your property, at no charge.

Do I need a valuation with my Level 3 Home Survey?

I've never understood why the highest-level survey doesn't include a valuation or a reinstatement value – it's supposed to be the most detailed. Although I don't think you need it, because if you're buying with a mortgage, the mortgage lender's valuation includes a reinstatement value. I believe, if the mortgage lender is happy with the price, then the price is right.

If you choose to bolt on a valuation, they cost from £50 to £200 on top. Personally, I wouldn't bother, I'd rely on the mortgage valuation instead.

How do I renegotiate?

Knowing how to negotiate the house price after a survey or a defect has been flagged by your solicitor can be challenging, as you'll not want to lose the property. Equally, you don't want to buy a property at full price if it is going to cost you thousands to repair after you move in.

In over 80% of house purchases the purchase price is negotiated at the outset, when you make your initial offer. Negotiating the house price *after* your survey may also be required, because:

• a defect has been found in your property survey such as damp or subsidence)[31]; or
• the mortgage lender's valuer has undervalued the property.

You might even feel that the seller was hiding something or that the estate agents were trying to get more for the property than it is worth. There is always the risk that the seller refuses your new offer and pulls out from the sale.

The goal is to base any reduction in your offer on actual numbers. If there is a defect, then get some quotes to fix it and include it with your email to the estate agent. Negotiations are best set out in an email first, so they have no emotion, and then they can be followed up by phone.

---

[31] 10 things that cause property values to decrease & how to fix them - https://www.samconveyancing.co.uk/news/conveyancing/10-things-that-cause-property-values-to-decrease

As we saw earlier in the book, all offers need to be presented to the seller – unless they have told their agent, in writing, that they will not receive offers below a certain amount. The seller will be upset they have a defect which will reduce their price.

This is a template email you can use. It is based on the facts, maintains a good relationship, and keeps the end goal in sight.

Dear [Estate Agent Name],

Re: [Property Address]

I hope you're ok. Things are progressing well for me with the conveyancing. My searches are back, enquiries are being finalised and I have completed my property survey; this final point has presented some issues that I need your help with.

The RICS surveyor has flagged up a number of issues that I was unaware of when I made my offer, and we need to discuss how best to proceed.

I'm sure you'll appreciate that when paying the current asking price of the property, I need to ensure that the property is in current market condition.

The following defects were raised:

• [List Defects]

I have spoken to 3 independent contractors, and they estimate the costs for making the repairs to be around £XXXX (I've attached their quotes).

The challenge is that any buyer will have these issues if they are looking to buy this property [and for some mortgage lenders they may not lend based on these defects.]

I am still very keen to buy the property and will be looking to exchange over the next few weeks, I ask that either the above items including the damp are addressed, or we agree to a reduction in the purchase price of £XXXX and I'll handle the repair works to the property after I move in.

I hope that we can move forward from here because I really want the house, however I can't afford to absorb these repair costs.

If the seller agrees to reduce the price it'll take me a few days to get my mortgage offer reissued to reflect the new price. So, the sooner we can get this agreed the better, as I don't want to hold up exchange because we are waiting for my mortgage lender.

I look forward to hearing back from you and the vendor by the [Date].

Kind regards,

[Your Name]

As with most negotiations, don't expect the seller or the estate agent to roll over straight away. There'll be some toing and froing as the seller wants the money and the agent wants their cut. If the cost to repair is high enough, then you need to decide: do you proceed and accept the additional cost? Or, do you dig in and send the following email:

Dear [Estate Agent Name],

Re: [Property Address]

Thank you for your help in reviewing the price of the property for us. Your help is appreciated.

I have thought about this at great length and feel that I cannot proceed with the purchase of the property at the original asking price based on the issues I have previously flagged in my letter dated the [Date].

Whilst we do still want to proceed with the purchase, we are rescinding our original offer and putting forward our revised offer of £XXX,XXX. This offer lasts until the [DATE]. If accepted, we will get the mortgage offer updated with an exchange as soon as it is returned. I have already signed all my exchange documents in anticipation for the seller's acceptance to the revised offer.

I hope this can be agreed by the seller as I'm sure they would prefer to complete this transaction in the next week or so, instead of the worry of finding a new buyer and then waiting another 8 weeks or more to get to completion.

I look forward to hearing back from you and the vendor by the [Date].

Kind regards,

[Your Name]

This shows that you are serious about halting the transaction until there is some concession. You may even have to pull your offer to show you are serious. The question that the seller needs to answer is: will they find a new buyer who won't be bothered about the issue (and how long are they prepared to wait to find one?) or do they agree to a discount and complete with you?

If worded well, you may find that you can successfully negotiate the seller down. But pride is something I've seen hinder negotiations, so keep that in mind and make sure the seller sees a win in accepting a lower offer. This is often an exchange ASAP.

CHAPTER 6

CONVEYANCING SEARCHES

What are conveyancing searches?

Information is held about your property by various sources. To access the information, you need to pay for the cost of the searches, usually through your solicitor, who will order the searches for you. Your solicitor will obtain the search results, review them, and raise questions upon the results of the report with the seller's solicitor, as is appropriate for your protection and that of your lender (if any).

The main searches are:

Primary Searches

1) **Local Authority Search** obtained from your local council. It contains information about planning applications and Building Control data on your property, rights of way, local controls, and restrictions. This is a mandatory search if you are getting a mortgage as a mortgage lender won't agree to lend without it, or (if applicable) without appropriate indemnity insurance. Council turnaround times vary from 3 days to 8 weeks.

2) **Water and Drainage search** obtained from your local water board. It contains information about where the water comes into the property, where your waste goes and if you're connected to a main line sewer. This is mandatory for most

lenders, although in practice all solicitors will obtain this search if you are buying with a mortgage.

3) **Environmental search** obtained from a search provider with information from various sources. It contains flood risk, ground stability, radon, contaminated land data and other environmental influencing factors.

4) **Chancel search** which identifies whether your property has a liability to pay for the upkeep of the local church (there was a case in 2003 which cost a homeowner almost £100,000[32])

Additional Searches

1) **Coal or Tin Mining** will reveal whether your property was built in a coal mining area and could therefore be affected by movement/subsidence.

2) **Contaminated Land enquiry**, if flagged as a risk in your environmental report then your solicitor conducts this enquiry with the council to confirm if your property was built on contaminated land.

3) **Radon search,** confirms whether the levels of radon in your area are high enough to necessitate further radon testing of potentially dangerous levels within the building itself. This mainly effects the Southwest of England but there are some higher readings in the Midlands.

4) **Flood Appraisal**, if flagged as a risk in your environmental report then you are required to have your property inspected for risk of being flooded.

---

[32] https://publications.parliament.uk/pa/ld200203/ldjudgmt/jd030626/aston-1.htm

Much like with surveys, your Primary Searches will identify whether you require any additional searches.

What are official and personal searches?

An official search is provided by the council and their costs vary but could be as high as £300. A personal search, also known as a regulated search, is provided by a search company who goes into the council and prepares the search for you. The cost is normally a lot cheaper and their turn around times can be faster.

The information should be the same whether you get an official or personal search. A personal search often comes with indemnity insurance to protect you in case there is any incorrect or missing information.

When should I order my searches?

You should order your searches once the chain is complete and once your solicitor receives the draft contract pack from the seller's solicitor. You might want to speed the process up by ordering them as soon as you instruct your solicitor, but you risk losing your money if the chain falls through, and you can no longer purchase the property.

How long do searches take to come back?

These are the turnaround times for the 4 primary searches:

- ✓ Local Authority Search. Depends on the local authority, Guildford Borough Council have a 3-day turnaround, but London Borough of Hackney have a 6-month turnaround time due to their systems being hacked.

- ✓ Water and Drainage Search. Depending on the waterboard it can take between 1 to 3 weeks.

- ✓ Environmental Search. 1 working day (normally same day).

✓   Chancel Search. 1 working day (normally same day).

I need to exchange but I don't have my local authority search back. What can I do?

You can obtain a Delayed Search Indemnity Policy through your solicitor. It is an insurance that you can't buy direct from the insurer as you are required to have legal advice from your solicitor on the terms of the policy.

The risks covered by search indemnity insurance vary between providers. The policy will generally cover any loss sustained because of adverse entries which would have been revealed, had a search been received prior to exchange of contracts. The loss is calculated to the value of any financial charge revealed in the search or as a reduction in market value of the property. i.e., if the information in the search results means the property isn't worth what you agreed to pay for it.

You can only obtain this insurance if you are unaware of the potential issue and if your mortgage lender will allow; not all do accept indemnity insurance. To check, you can go to the UK Finance Lenders' Handbook for Conveyancers and search for your lender under *Part 1 and 2* – it tells you in *Section 5.4.6 Does the lender accept search insurance and, if yes, what are the lender's specific requirements?*[33]

While search indemnity insurance provides some cover in case of damage to the property, it offers no protection to the buyer's quality of living once they have moved into the property. For example, moving into a property which is liable to heavy flooding or subsidence may be difficult to live with and cause issues with selling the property in the future.

---

[33] https://lendershandbook.ukfinance.org.uk/lenders-handbook/

Skipping a search for insurance instead may also mean that you miss an issue, which had you known, would have prevented you from buying the property at all.

For example, if there is a planned road or railway being built near your property, that'll make the property less valuable. Alternatively, you may have had plans to cut some trees down to let in more light, a local search may reveal that the trees are subject to a tree preservation order and that cutting them down is prohibited.

Which searches are mandatory for my mortgage lender?

Most solicitors choose to obtain the Primary Searches; some mortgage lenders will want more, or less. Every lender has their own position on what searches they need and what information in those searches needs to be reported to them.

To find out what your mortgage lender requires, go to the UK Finance Lenders' Handbook for Conveyancers and search for your lender under *Part 1 and 2* – it tells you in:

- ✓ 5.4.4 Does the lender want to receive environmental or contaminated land reports?

- ✓ 5.4.5 Does the lender accept personal searches and, if yes, what are the lender's requirements?

- ✓ 5.5.3b Does the lender require an original/copy of the planning permission?

- ✓ 5.5.3c Does the lender require an original/copy of the building regulation consents?

- ✓ 5.5.3d Does the lender require certificates of lawful use or development/established use certificate?

I'm a cash buyer, do I need searches?

If you're fortunate to purchase without a mortgage, I recommend you obtain at least the primary searches, but as a cash buyer you can choose not to.

Without them, you may miss issues that would put you off buying the property, or you may find that you should have gotten the property at a much-reduced purchase price, to accommodate the money it will cost you to rectify the problems.

You'd kick yourself, if when you came to sell, your buyer got searches, they found an issue, and then drove you down on the sale price. For the sake of £200-£400 the property searches should be a necessity, not a cost saver. If a lender won't lend without searches, then why should you take the risk?

CHAPTER 7

CONTRACTS AND ENQUIRIES

Contracts and enquiries
What are draft contracts?
The seller prepares the draft contract pack, which includes the legal documents your solicitor will review to assess any risks with purchasing this property, for you and your mortgage lender. The draft contract pack includes:

1) **Contract of Sale** – this states the property you're buying, the names of the seller and buyer, the purchase price, and the contents you are buying. It'll include the standard conditions for sale plus any other amendments.

   A contract of sale will be hand amended by your solicitor to correct mistakes within it. This is very normal, especially if there is a spelling error in your name or the address. The seller's solicitor uses the sales memorandum to draft the contract so if it is wrong there, then you'll be sure to find it drafted incorrectly by the seller's solicitor.

   You can ask for the seller to update the contract, they often decline as it isn't required. It is simpler and easier to hand amend the contract. Although, any errors with the TR1 must be amended as we see below.

2) **Seller's Property Information Forms** (SPIF also known as the protocol forms)

   a. **TA6 Property Information Form** includes information about your neighbours, alterations, and things that your seller knows have affected your property during their ownership.

   b. **TA10 Fittings and Contents Form** includes what is sold as part of the sale price, what is being taken and what is up for sale in addition, that you may choose to buy or ask them to take. If it doesn't state that an item is included within this form, don't expect to see it in the property when you move in. Make sure any verbal agreements for white goods are correct in this document.

   And, if leasehold:

   c. **TA7 Leasehold Information Form** includes who your freeholder is, whether there is a managing agent, ground rent or service charges, and other leasehold information that the seller knows.

   d. **Leasehold Management Pack** is provided by the freeholder, and/or managing agent, and is sent 2 to 8 weeks after you get your offer accepted. It includes ground rent and service charge statements, financial statements and planned major works, and other leasehold management information.

   e. **Deed of Covenant** (if required by the lease).

   f. **Licence to Assign.** Some leases (albeit a minority) also require a Leaseholder to obtain the Freeholders' consent to sell the property. To obtain the Freeholders consent, the seller of the leasehold may have to provide some information about you, the buyer. You will have to pay for the Freeholder to provide a Licence to Assign, which could be up to £400.00 + VAT.

3) **Official Copy of the Register**

4) **Original Transfer/Conveyance**

5) **Title Plan**

6) **Warranties and Guaranties**

7) **EPC**

The contracts are called drafts because the buyer's solicitor makes amendments to the contract for any changes they feel are required.

What's the delay with draft contracts?

To understand what the delay is, we need to understand what the seller needs to do before their solicitor can issue contracts. Here is a list of what needs to be done before contracts can be issued:

1) Seller finds and instructs their solicitor. You'll know once this is done because the estate agent will issue a Sales Memorandum which includes the contact details for the buyer's and seller's solicitors.

2) The seller completes the Seller's Property Information Forms (SPIF, also known as the Protocol Forms). These include:

    a.   TA6 Property Information Form
    b.   TA10 Fittings and Contents Form

    c.   (If leasehold) TA7 Leasehold Information Form

They add up to around 30 pages, in total, for the seller to complete. The seller can often find it hard to compile all the information in one go as they look to source it from various places.

This is further delayed if the transaction involves the sale of a property owned by a person who has died (a probate sale) or the sale is by a person who has lost mental capacity (a sale under a Power of Attorney) as they often can't locate the documents being requested. Once completed, the seller sends the documents to their solicitor in the post. All this process takes somewhere between 1 to 2 weeks (sometimes longer), plus days lost for snail mail.

Some seller's solicitors have digital SPIFs that can be completed and signed online, and they'll accept scanned documents through an online portal or via email which is a huge time saver.

3) The buyer's solicitor emails the seller's solicitor, confirming they are instructed and await the draft contract pack.

4) The seller's solicitor prepares the draft contract and TR1 and sends these to the buyer's solicitor.

I've found the best way to speed this process up is to inform the estate agent that the contracts have not been received and get them to chase the seller, as the agent is already motivated toward a faster completion.

What are enquiries?
This is where your solicitor earns their fee, as they'll review the draft contracts and look for any legal issues with the paperwork that require investigation. Each question they have is known as a

legal enquiry.

For a freehold there'll be somewhere in the region of 5 to 10 enquiries and a leasehold will have 15 to 20. If there are any more enquiries than this, then either the seller has provided very limited information in the draft contracts, or your solicitor is being very thorough and diligent in making sure all the "I's" are dotted and "t's" crossed!

An enquiry may even be a question you have, after reviewing the Property Information Forms or after viewing the property, such as:

1) Are the white goods being left in the property as part of the sale price?
2) Can you complete on the 31st of October?
3) Where is the parking for the property?

These types of enquiries are what I call "personal preference" or "part of the deal" as they are things that mean something to you or have been agreed between you and the seller. Your solicitor will get answers to these questions for you and bind the seller into the answer.

As I flagged earlier in *Chapter 1 – WARNING – Beware direct communication with the seller!* anything you agree with the seller needs to be confirmed between your solicitor and their solicitor. Get this wrong and you'll be left frustrated if you don't get what you thought you had agreed.

What enquiries are deal breakers?
There are hundreds of different enquiries, some are nice to haves, and some are deal breakers.

To clarify the latter, a deal breaker is where you can't get a mortgage unless the enquiry is satisfied, so unless you can afford to buy the property with no mortgage, then the deal is dead, and you need to start hunting for a new property to buy. Cash buyers can ignore any deal breaker and buy the property with any unsatisfied enquiry, no matter how bad it is, but they must accept that the property could be difficult to re-sell or mortgage.

Here's some of the top enquiries, whether they are dealbreakers, and what needs to be done to resolve them:

Freehold enquiries

Enquiry	Works completed without being signed off and registered at building control.
What is it?	Works including removal of load bearing walls, extensions and Part B electrical works require building control sign off, to confirm the work meets Building Control standards. These works are registered at building control and will appear within your local authority search.
Is it a deal breaker?	You either: 1) Get the seller to have the works signed off so you know they are safe and do meet building control standards; or 2) Obtain indemnity insurance to protect your lender if the value of the property goes down, if the council require the works to be removed/rectified. The cost depends on the property value, ranging between £100 and £1,000. You can ask the seller to pay for the indemnity insurance. It is a deal breaker if you aren't prepared to get indemnity insurance, if your lender does not accept

indemnity insurance, or if the council are already aware of the works.

Enquiry	Updates to the contract of sale.
What is it?	The seller's solicitor drafts the contract, and they can often mis-spell names, addresses, and even have the wrong purchase price.
Is it a deal breaker?	Not a deal breaker and these changes could be made by hand, by you or your solicitor.

Enquiry	Breach of a restrictive covenant.
What is it?	A restrictive covenant is a condition set out within your title which the owner of the freehold must adhere to. You can get some very old ones such as "you must not use the property as a farm" or "store pigs", or more current ones such as "you are only allowed to have one dwelling on the title".
	The condition was applied to the title when the land was originally sold off, so if you breach it then it needs to be remedied, or you'll need the consent of the original transferor to amend the covenant. If the latter, trying to find the party to contact to ask their permission is hard, as they are often dead, and you'll need to find their beneficiaries.
	If the seller or any previous owner has breached a

	covenant, you could become liable for their breach, which is why this enquiry is raised.
Is it a deal breaker?	You either: 1) Get the seller to remedy the breach; or 2) Obtain indemnity insurance to protect your lender in the event that the value of the property goes down, if the original transferor requires the breach to be remedied. The cost depends on the property value ranging between £100 to £1,000. You can ask the seller to pay for the indemnity insurance, or if indemnity insurance is not available, to remedy the breach. It is a deal breaker if you aren't prepared to get indemnity insurance or remedy the breach.
Enquiry	Who's responsible for maintaining the fence?
What is it?	Most title plans have the boundaries marked on them. It is then stated within the deed who maintains the different boundaries.
Is it a deal breaker?	It isn't a deal breaker for your lender. You should still check that boundaries that you will become responsible for aren't in an unacceptable condition, in case you can't afford to renew them. I'd even check the ones you aren't responsible for, because if they've been left to get into a bad state then you may have a battle with your new neighbours to get them fixed.

Enquiry	Japanese Knotweed
What is it?	Spotted during your viewing, by your surveyor, or flagged in the Property Information Forms, this intrusive weed can cause damage to your property.
Is it a deal breaker?	The issue will need to be reported to your lender. If they agree to lend, then you need to decide if you'll take on the removal of the weed. The cost to remove is considerable and you need specialist contractors to remove it.

Enquiry	Boundary dispute.
What is it?	Check your title plan matches what your actual boundary looks like. You can often find the physical boundary and legal boundary changes over time.
Is it a deal breaker?	Resolving an issue can be difficult. If the argument is with a neighbour encroaching your land, then you may find this mentioned within the TA6 Form.

Enquiry	Access to your property.
What is it?	Does your title plan connect to the road, or do you have to cross over someone's land to get to your property?
Is it a	If you don't have direct access to get to your

deal breaker?	property you are trespassing to get to it, so your solicitor needs to investigate if you have a right of access to pass over that land. In most cases there is an agreement already in place. If not, your solicitor may need to contact the landowner to obtain their consent.

Check Section 8.2-3 in the TA6 to see if the seller is aware of any access issues. |

Leasehold enquiries

Enquiry	The lease has a doubling ground rent clause.
What is it?	Some leases contain ground rent clauses that double after a set number of years (10/15/20 years). Once the rent exceeds a certain amount, then your lease is seen as an Assured Shorthold Tenancy, not a leasehold.

New leases are subject to ground rent caps as per leaseholder protections 2022 |
| *Is it a deal breaker?* | The seller needs to contact the freeholder and obtain their consent to vary the lease (using a deed of variation) and replace the rental clause with one that your mortgage lender will allow. The legal costs and premium payable to the freeholder need to be paid for by either you or the seller.

It is a deal breaker if your lender won't agree to the ground rent clause and the freeholder won't change it. |

Enquiry	The lease doesn't allow pets.
What is it?	Most leaseholds prohibit you from having pets in the property.
Is it a deal breaker?	You can ask for the freeholder to remove the clause via a deed of variation, this is at their discretion, and if agreed, the legal work will be at your own cost.
	Some leases will allow pets on the proviso that they do not cause a nuisance or annoyance to other owners/ occupiers in the building. Beware, you could be asked to remove your pets if the neighbours complain.
	If the freeholder won't budge on their position, then you need to you need to decide how much you like your pets, for me it'd be a deal breaker.

Enquiry	Major works.
What is it?	Where your freeholder is planning major works, and these have yet to be undertaken and/or paid for, then you are buying a lease with a considerable financial cost associated to it.
	You'll find out what major works are in the pipeline within the leasehold information pack provided by the seller. There may be a Section 20 Notice which states what works are required. Under Section 20 of

the Landlord & Tenant Act 1985 it states that freeholders must consult with leaseholders if works are set to cost any one leaseholder more than £250.

See 'Does the lease qualify for leaseholder protections?' below for safety remediation costs.

Is it a deal breaker?	If there are major works planned, then these will be referred to your mortgage lender, to confirm if they are prepared to lend. If they are, then you need to decide if you can afford to pay for the major works. It is common practise to reduce your offer by some, or even all, of the cost of the works. It is a deal breaker if your lender doesn't agree to lend or if you can't afford to pay for the works.

Enquiry	Short lease.
What is it?	Mortgage lenders require your lease to have a minimum number of unexpired years. Different lenders allow different lengths, for some the limit is 80 years, others 70, very few will accept shorter leases.
Is it a deal breaker?	If the remaining term falls under what your lender will allow, then you'll need to get the lease extended, or it is a deal breaker.

Only the seller can extend the lease and you can do this formally[34] or informally[35].

Whichever route you go down, this is going to add months onto your conveyancing process, and you'll need to agree who is paying the costs.

Enquiry	EWS1 Form.
What is it?	A block of flats over 18 metres is required to have an EWS1 Form to confirm the type of cladding used on the external parts of the property.
Is it a deal breaker?	If there is no EWS1 Form, then you'll need to wait until the freeholder obtains this. There are very few surveyors who offer the service so it could take a few months to obtain. If the EWS1 Form shows the property has cladding that is combustible, then this needs to be referred to your mortgage lender and is most likely a deal breaker unless you are a Qualifying Leaseholder in a

---

[34] Formal Lease Extension - https://www.samconveyancing.co.uk/news/conveyancing/lease-extension-process-3772
[35] Informal Lease Extension - https://www.samconveyancing.co.uk/news/conveyancing/informal-lease-extension-process-what-are-the-pros-cons-6015

relevant building. Even then, there are only a select few lenders who are currently willing to lend on these properties.

Enquiry	Does the lease qualify for leaseholder protections?
What is it?	Leaseholder protections[36] came into force with The Building Safety Act 2022. Qualifying leaseholders are protected from the financial burden of remediation costs concerning unsafe cladding for Flats over 11 meters high (from the lowest point to the top floor). For non-cladding safety remediation, these costs are capped and must be spread over 10 years. Without protections, you may become liable for the lease's full share of any of these costs which may arise after purchase.
Is it a deal breaker?	You need to be provided with a Deed of Certificate, to confirm the protections pass to you as the new owner to avoid the costs of repair being passed onto you.

Enquiry	Parking.
What is it?	Does your flat come with parking? If it doesn't where will you park your car? Is there space for 2

36

	cars?
Is it a deal breaker?	Parking restrictions apply in many major towns and cities so knowing where you can park your car is important. You may need to pay for private parking or apply to the council for a resident permit. The Section 9 of the TA6 is states if the property has any parking and if it is in a controlled parking zone or within a local authority parking scheme.

You can view even more legal enquiries online[37].

No reply, get indemnity insurance?
There is an indemnity insurance for pretty much any issues that crop up during legal enquiries stage. It could be for:

> ➤ The seller removed a load bearing wall but didn't get the work signed off at Building Control.

> ➤ The seller has installed a boiler which isn't registered at Gas Safety or at Building Control.

> ➤ The seller, or a previous seller, has built an extension which has breached a restrictive covenant.

Whilst buying with cash you can ignore these issues, but when buying with a mortgage, you can't. The mortgage lender requires either the issue to be remedied or an indemnity policy to protect their mortgage debt if the property goes down in value because of the issue.

---

[37] https://www.samconveyancing.co.uk/news/conveyancing/what-are-legal-enquiries-3432

The problem with indemnity insurance is that it sweeps the issue under the carpet and doesn't fix it. Yes, it gets you to completion and into the property, but you're left with the problem to fix.

You take on both the cost and the risk. What if the boiler wasn't installed properly and there is a gas leak which starts a fire? What if removing the load-bearing wall has made the property structurally unsafe and part of the building collapses? What if the previous landowner forces you to take down your extension? These are the risks and costs you're taking on by ignoring the issue and just obtaining indemnity insurance. It doesn't pay for you to fix the issue, it just protects the mortgage lender.

You'll sleep better at night if you get the seller to correct the issue before you buy the property. On occasions though, the pressure of the process takes over and you accept the indemnity route in a hope you won't have a problem whilst you live there or when you come to sell. The latter issue could mean a future buyer pushes you down on the sale price because of the risk.

What are reasonable times to wait for stuff to get done?

There are different stages that take different lengths of time, and it often doesn't matter how much you chase, the time it takes doesn't change (although you are left frustrated and stressed from fruitless effort). To save you the hassle, here are some standard turnaround times for different stages in the process – I'll include some ways to speed them up:

1) **Local Authority Search**. The time to get this depends on your council. Call them up and ask for their current turnaround time. It can range between 3 and 180 days (or more). To speed the process up, order your searches on instruction and ask if the council have an expedited service. The latter comes at a cost, and one I think is not worth

paying.

2) **Contracts are in**, when will my solicitor raise enquiries? This process is known as title checking and solicitors work on a first in first out basis for their work. Expect to wait between 5 to 7 working days for your solicitor to complete their title check.

   There isn't a way to speed this up, however you can slow it down by calling and emailing them a lot asking when they'll raise enquiries. The less time your solicitor spends "fielding emails" and answering the phone, the quicker they can get on with the important work. If you really want some assurance, call, and ask to speak your solicitor's secretary, they will either know the position or find it out for you.

3) **Mortgage offer**. After application, getting your formal mortgage offer can take 2 to 6 weeks.

4) **Replies to enquiries**. As a rule, it takes the seller's solicitor 1 to 2 weeks on a freehold and 2 to 4 weeks on a leasehold to reply to a buyer's legal enquiries. If there is an enquiry requiring replies from the freeholder, council or any third party then expect for this process to drag on beyond the rule above. Ways to speed this process up would be to set deadlines, where you'll pull or reduce your offer price if the seller is unable to provide replies to the enquiries.

   You should also use the selling agent to help keep the pressure on the seller and keep you updated as to the progress with the replies. Sadly, this phase can often be a waiting game, my best advice is to understand the enquiry, know whose job it is to get the reply, and be reasonable in how long you expect for the reply to be answered.

What is the most efficient way to get an update?

Most clients will call and then be disappointed that they can't get through to their solicitor. Or, if they do, then the solicitor needs to review the file before they can come back to them. It can be frustrating. There is a reason, and I can either sugar coat it, or tell you as it is:

"You're not their only client".

Solicitors are like doctors; they have many clients and before they can comment on your question, they need to review their notes and the last correspondence. For solicitors this could mean checking an online file, for most it'll mean going to their filing cabinet and pulling out your paper file.

With anywhere between 60 to 120 clients your solicitor won't be able to remember exactly where you are at the very time you call, especially if they are in the middle of raising enquiries on another client's file or if they're trying to finalise an exchange of contracts.

To avoid this frustration and get the answer you need, the most efficient way to get an update is to email your solicitor and copy in their assistant. Here's a good example:

Hi Solicitor,

I hope you're ok. When last we spoke on the 15th of November 2022 you told me we were waiting on replies to enquiries from the seller's solicitor.

Please can you confirm if you have now had replies in from the seller's solicitor? If they are, were the enquiries satisfactory to allow you to report out to me with documents for signing? If you can confirm either way with a quick email back, then I can help get this chased.

I have copied in your assistant in case they can check the file to save you time. I've also copied in the estate agent just in case they are aware of any delays with the seller replying as I'm keen to move forward to achieve a completion date of the 30th of November.

If you could reply to me before this Friday, it'd be much appreciated. If I don't hear from you, I'll give your office a call.

You're giving your solicitor time to read and reply, reminding them of the completion date you want and copying in the estate agent so they can help chase the seller's solicitor for you.

If you don't hear back from your solicitor by Friday, then call them on the phone. Whether you get through or not, they'll receive your missed call and know they need to respond to you otherwise you'll call again.

How do you protect yourself when buying with someone else?

Whilst buying a property with someone else makes buying a house more affordable, it throws up complications if you fall out with them. Who pays the mortgage if one of you must move out? What do you do if one person wants to sell, and the other doesn't? How do you stop arguments over who gets what when you sell? Or protect against losing the family home after a divorce.

The good news is that prior planning, agreeing, and documenting the principles for these eventualities can make disagreements easier to cope with. In this section I'll answer all the above questions and explain the kay parts to co-owning a property. I'll summarise a lot because there's another book in this series coming soon, which will explore all these options in depth.

Different ownership for different relationships

When you purchase a house, you need to state in the Land Registry Transfer document (TR1) how you will hold the property, as joint tenants, or tenants in common. How you hold the property and the protections you need depends on the relationship you have with the co-owner/s.

- **Married.** Most married couples buy as joint tenants because they want the reassurance of knowing if either of them dies, their share of the property stays with the surviving spouse. As tenants in common, the share of the property would go to the deceased's estate and could cause complications for the surviving spouse. If you divorce then the property, along with all your other assets and liabilities, will be lumped together and you, a mediator, or the courts sort out who gets what and if/when the property should be sold.

- **Unmarried Partners.** You may choose to buy as joint tenants with a plan to get married. If you break up prior to marriage, you risk a legal battle to prove what you earn and how to sell; especially when you're throwing insults at each other because one of you has cheated.

  This can be avoided by buying as tenants in common, whereby you both own a percentage share of the beneficial interest, and if you break up, your share is yours. To protect you even further, draft a deed of trust (see next section).

- **Family.** You might think that buying with family is a safe bet; "blood is thicker than water", and all that, but be careful because relationships breakdown, even in families. Plus, what happens if one of the owners gets married? Their partner might try and make a claim to the property. If they divorce, then the divorcees share of the property is most likely to be included in the divorce settlement and the property may have to be sold as part of the divorce.

  The best advice is to buy as tenants in common and draft a deed of trust.

What is a deed of trust?

In simple terms it's a contract whereby the owners agree the principles about the property and the money. It'll most likely include:

- ✓ What percentage you each own of the beneficial interest (your equity/money).

- ✓ What happens if one of you wants to sell?

- ✓ How to buy the other owner's beneficial interest to avoid selling.

This is all included in a simple deed of trust[38]. You can get more complex deeds to cover a variety of future events. The objective is always to agree the principles at the outset, when the going is good, and then use the deed in the event of a disagreement.

If an owner chooses to ignore the terms of the deed, much like any legal agreement, it is easier to enforce and remedy the issue. A deed is a very formal document, and your signatures are witnessed so the Courts will see this as an open and shut case if you try and dispute what is in the deed.

You should make sure you take legal advice on the deed of trust to ensure you are happy with what you are agreeing to.

What happens if you don't have a deed of trust?

It gets very messy if you break up and argue. Most of the time one person wants to sell and get their money and the other

---

[38] https://www.samconveyancing.co.uk/news/conveyancing/deed-of-trust-4378

doesn't[39]. You then have the argument of: How much of the sale proceeds are you due?

Whilst you can force a sale, to do so can cost upward of £20,000 and you may not be successful; especially if the property is a family home with children in it. When you apply for an order, the Courts could rule any of the following:

- refuse a sale,

- refuse a sale but make an order regulating the right to occupy the property,

- order a sale,

- order a sale but suspend the order for a short period; and

- partition the co-owned property (only awarded in exceptional cases).

Be careful who moves into your property!

If you bought your house on your own and then allowed a partner to move in, and they start paying money towards the property (mortgage repayments, household costs, repairs/maintenance) then they could make a claim on the beneficial interest. It's known as a constructive trust which means you could be holding the legal title on trust for someone who moved in and is getting a beneficial interest by paying money toward the house.

To avoid this, you can:

---

[39] https://www.samconveyancing.co.uk/news/conveyancing/can-i-force-the-sale-of-a-jointly-owned-property-6179

1) Get a solicitor to draft a declaration of no interest. This is a legal document which confirms the person living in the property has no rights to the property.

2) Sign an occupier waiver form. This is mandatory for a mortgage lender for anyone who is 16 years old and over who lives at the property. It confirms they have no legal right to the property.

   The mortgage lender doesn't want the hassle of a resident in the property claiming they have a right to be there if they have to repossess.

3) Put in writing that the payments being made are equivalent to rent and don't give a beneficial interest in the property. If this is your partner then as unromantic as this sounds, it offers some protection.

   If the payments are large and over a long period of time this may not be strong enough evidence. For example, a court would be less likely to believe that your partner paid for you to have an extension on your house (increasing its value) and did not expect to get anything back.

4) Confirm the money is a loan and agree how you will pay the money back.

CHAPTER 8

EXCHANGE OF CONTRACTS

What do I need to sign?

Once your solicitor has satisfied all the legal enquiries then they'll prepare a Report on Title and provide you with documents to sign. The Report on Title sets out all the information your solicitor has obtained relating to your property and should be read in conjunction with the seller's property information/documentation.

The Report on Title doesn't say, "you are fine to buy this property", it doesn't give any opinion. The objective is to inform you of everything the solicitor has found out about the property, so that you can make an informed decision as to whether to proceed with the purchase of the property or not.

If you are happy to proceed, you can sign and return to your solicitor:

1) **Contract of sale.** This just needs signing – no witnesses and don't date it. Some solicitors can now do this digitally. Things to check are: your name is in full, correct property address, property price and address. Any amendments can be made by hand by you – all contracts get written on and amended like this so not to worry it doesn't have to be typed up perfectly but does need to have the correct

information on it.

2) **TR1 Form**. You need to sign and get the signing witnessed – don't date it. Some solicitors can now do this digitally. Once again check all the details as above.

3) **Stamp Duty Land Tax Declaration Form**. This just needs signing – no witnesses and don't date. Some solicitors can now do this digitally and a form needs to be filed even if there is no tax to be paid (if there is consideration being paid).

4) **Mortgage Deed**. You need to sign and get the signing witnessed. We expect the Land Registry to begin allowing digital signatures on this deed at some point in 2023-24.

5) **(If leasehold) Deed of Covenant or other deeds**. You need to sign and get the signing witnessed – don't date it.

6) **(If freehold) Buildings Insurance.** Some solicitors like to see sight of your building insurance policy for your new home on the day of completion.

The signed documents need to be sent back to your solicitor in the post by special delivery. Recorded Delivery only allows you to track the documents, whereas Special Delivery guarantees their arrival. I would suggest scanning them across to your solicitor so they can review them and pick up on any errors, but the originals go in the post.

The solicitor can't exchange without all your signed documents, so make sure to send them back ASAP!

Should I sign even though we're not ready?
The signing and returning of the documents don't bind you into the purchase until your solicitor exchanges contracts. This logistical

stage can take weeks, so it helps to get the paperwork signed and out of the way. If you want to save time, sign the documents and return them with a note that the solicitor can't exchange without your consent. The latter is the case in any event, but I mention to put your mind at rest.

You may prefer to wait until all enquiries are satisfied and then sign your documents and send them to your solicitor. Exchange of contracts will be delayed until your signed documents are in.

What happens if the purchase falls through?

Whilst it may come as a shock if the seller pulls out, you can often save a purchase even after it has fallen through. You need to first find out why. Here are some of the most common reasons for the seller or the buyer to pull out and how to get things back on track:

The seller is fed up with waiting.

Sellers can often get frustrated if they are left in limbo and not kept up to speed with where you are in the process. There are many reasons for this including:

- ✓ There was a delay with obtaining your mortgage offer.
- ✓ There was a delay with obtaining your property searches.
- ✓ Your solicitor is slow.
- ✓ There is a legal argument between the seller's and buyer's solicitors where they can't agree on a legal point.

If you are still keen to buy the property, the seller needs to know:

1) Why is there a delay;
2) What will fix it;
3) Reminder that completing with you is faster than any other buyer; and
4) (If all else fails) an additional incentive to rescue the deal: cash or deadline.

Here is an example email you can send to the estate agent to rescue the deal:

Hi [Estate Agent Name],

Thank you for letting me know the seller is frustrated and wants to pull the purchase. I am equally frustrated with the process and want to get into the property as soon as possible.

I've spoken to my solicitor, and they have confirmed the delay relates to XXXX.

They've agreed that to progress, what we need to do is XXXX.

I understand the seller is frustrated with the wait and I'm sorry if they didn't know the above is what is outstanding. Would the seller be prepared to carry on if we set a deadline for exchange, of the 31st of August? Alternatively, is there a completion date the seller would prefer to achieve after this (my solicitor said a minimum of 5 days post is needed)?

I'm not sure if the seller will agree to this, however if they are still selling the property then it is unlikely they'll find another buyer and get to this stage before the deadline above. This'll leave the seller waiting longer to complete.

I really like the property and want to carry on with the purchase. Now the seller knows what the bottle neck is, and we have a deadline in place, shall we focus on getting the above issue addressed and get the purchase over the line?

Please let me know what the seller says and as always thank you for your help.

What is exchange of contracts?

It is the best day ever! I never understand the fixation with completion because whilst you collect your keys and have the back breaking task of moving in, the actual day when the stress and worry of it all falling through lifts away, is exchange of contracts.

The process to exchange contracts is as follows:

1) Pre-exchange checks completed by your solicitor including:
    a. Obtain your consent to exchange (required on each new day, so even if given today, if you don't exchange you need to give consent again tomorrow) normally via email,
    b. Bankruptcy search on you,
    c. Priority is applied at the Land Registry (stops anyone else doing something to the title between now and when the property is registered in your name),
    d. Confirm mortgage funds can be released in time for completion,
    e. Prepare the certificate of title to submit to lender to draw down mortgage funds for completion (submitted after exchange),
    f. Receive the Replies to Requisitions from the seller's solicitor. It contains the seller's solicitor's bank details and lists out the undertakings such as providing vacant possession.

2) Solicitor informs the chain they are ready to exchange.

3) Seller's solicitor calls your solicitor, and they confirm the:
    a. names of seller and buyer
    b. title number
    c. property address
    d. chattels/fittings and contents included in or in addition to the purchase price.
    e. purchase price
    f. deposit to be paid (normally 10%) and whether to

be sent by cheque or held to order (unless agreed otherwise in the contract, this is held by your solicitor. In some cases, the seller will request that the deposit is sent to be held by their solicitor instead)

g. completion date (either a set date or on notice)

4) The time and date are noted on the contracts.

Contracts are now exchanged and neither seller nor buyer can pull out without incurring financial penalties.

What is an exchange on notice?

When you purchase a new build that hasn't yet been built, you'll exchange contracts but there won't be a date stated for completion. Once the construction is complete and signed off, the developer will serve you notice to complete on your purchase. You then have 10 working days to do so.

You'll often have a long stop date written into the contract which allows you to break from the contract without penalties if you don't get served notice to complete by a specific date.

Who can witness a signature?

Who Can	Who Can't
✓ A friend not connected to the transaction. ✓ Neighbours. ✓ Work colleagues. ✓ Flat mate.	✗ Anyone in your family. ✗ Anyone named on the mortgage. ✗ Anyone providing a gift. ✗ Anyone connected to the purchase such as the estate agent or mortgage broker.

What happens if I pull out after exchange?

This is one of the most read articles on the SAM Conveyancing website, despite being incredibly unlikely, because of the penalties for pulling out at this stage. Plus, on exchange of contracts you will have given your authority to exchange so it is unlikely after all the toing and froing with questions during the process that you'll even want to pull out.

What happens if the buyer pulls out after exchange?

If the buyer pulls out after exchange of contracts, then most contracts of sale state:

7.4 Buyer's failure to comply with notice to complete
7.4.1 If the buyer fails to complete in accordance with a notice to complete, the following terms apply.

7.5.2 The seller may rescind the contract, and if he does so:
   a) he may:
      i.   forfeit and keep any deposit and accrued interest
      ii. resell the property and any contents included in the contract
      iii. claim damages

   b) the buyer is to return any documents he received from the seller and is to cancel any registration of the contract.

7.4.3 The seller retains his other rights and remedies.

What happens if the seller pulls out after exchange?

If the seller pulls out after exchange of contracts, then most contracts of sale state:

7.5 Seller's failure to comply with notice to complete
7.5.1   If the seller fails to complete in accordance with a

notice to complete, the following terms apply.

7.5.2   The buyer may rescind the contract, and if he does so:

> a) *the deposit is to be repaid to the buyer with accrued interest*
> b) *the buyer is to return any documents he received from the seller and is, at the seller's expense, to cancel any registration of the contract.*

7.5.3   The buyer retains his other rights and remedies.

How long between exchange and completion?

You can agree any timeframe with your seller from 1 week to 6 months. The most common time frame is 1 week because it gives both you and the seller time to pack your boxes. Plus, you don't have the worry of anything changing between exchange and completion.

Here are some examples of alternate timeframes and reasons for them:

- **2 months** because you want to hand in your notice on your rental property and are trying to avoid paying rent and mortgage repayments at the same time. Whilst it is nice to have a perfect notice time that links to your completion day, it helps having a week overlap. It makes the day of completion less hectic. You can take the week to move from your rental to your new home and make sure the rental is clean and tidy, so you get your full deposit back from your landlord.

- **Same day exchange and completion** is also known as a simultaneous exchange and completion. This should be a last resort because it applies too much pressure on all parties in the chain and has a huge risk of not completing. You are reliant on the mortgage coming in, your pre-exchange and pre-completion checks all being ok, then there is the pressure on the seller to move out so you can move in. Most sellers don't pack until they know exchange is going to happen because they don't want to live out of boxes, so having no time in-between exchange and completion creates huge time pressure.

Common reasons for having to complete on the same day would be if your mortgage offer is going to expire or if the seller has threatened to pull out if a specific date isn't achieved.

What is the LMS portal for mortgage lenders?

LMS is an online portal that some mortgage lenders require your solicitor to use, to download your mortgage offer, occupier waiver form and to submit an E-COT (electronic certificate of title sent to draw down your mortgage). If your lender requires you to use the LMS portal, you will be liable for the LMS fee of £35 plus VAT; this is not a solicitor fee and is mandatory if you use one of the lenders below:

Atom Bank Plc, Bluestone, Buckinghamshire Building Society, Chorley Building Society, Clydesdale and Yorkshire Bank, Cynergy, Danske Bank, Darlington Building Society, Dudley Building Society, Hinckley & Rugby Building Society, HSBC Bank Plc, Investec Bank, Leeds Building Society, LiveMore Capital, Marsden Building Society, Melton Building Society, Monmouthshire Building Society, National Westminster Bank Plc, Newcastle Building Society, Royal Bank of Scotland Plc, Skipton Building Society, TSB Bank Plc, Virgin Money Plc, and West Bromwich Building Society.

More mortgage lenders are using LMS so expect to see this list grow.

You are liable for Building Insurance from exchange.

On a freehold you are liable to have building insurance in place from the day of exchange, not completion. This means you need to have your policy ready to take out on the day your solicitor is ready to exchange contracts.

When getting a quote, you'll need to answer some questions about the property such as:

- How and when was the property constructed?
- What locks and alarms are on the property?
- What is the reinstatement value of the property?

If you don't know the answer to some of these then ask your RICS surveyor or your estate agent to check with the seller. If the information isn't correct, then your insurer may not pay out in the event of a claim. Once you move in, you should update the policy with any updates that you find, as soon as possible, to ensure you are covered.

For a leasehold you only need contents insurance. It is still a good idea to double check what the freeholder's building insurance covers. Some insurance policies cover the walls in the flat, but not the tiles on the walls. If you have a flood, then you may find your cover won't include the cost of retiling. If this is the case speak to your insurance providers to get contents insurance that covers this.

Can I get access between exchange and completion?

The seller's solicitor hates this type of request because there is no upside for the seller, unless you pay them for it, but there is a downside. If you fail to complete, trying to get you to move out is problematic.

The upside for you is mainly so you can move your stuff in or get some works done prior to moving in. There is no hard and fast rule on making the seller agree to the access so ask and see what they say. You might even build it into your offer at the beginning – "I'll offer asking price if I can have access between exchange and completion".

If the seller is worried you might damage the property, then you can let them know that you are liable for the insurance for the property from exchange of contracts (on freeholds, for flats the freeholder has the building insurance). If you're having improvement works done, then they will gain the benefit of the works if the purchase falls through.

Hire a van or get removals?

With all the costs of the purchase, hiring a removals company may feel like a thing you can save money on. It was for me. When I moved into my first home in 2001, I hired a white van and my brothers helped get all of my stuff into the flat (ground floor, much harder lugging your stuff upstairs – ever seen that scene in Friends with the sofa on the stairs? Pivot![40]).

On my next purchase, in 2014, I decided to save my back and hired a removals company to pack, unpack and rebuild. Best money I ever spent because it meant we completed on the Friday and we were living in the property like normal from the Monday. No boxes unpacked. I will never now not use a removals company.

If you choose to use a removals company for your move, then here are a few things you need to do:

- ✓ The pack, unpack and rebuild service comes as an additional cost so find out what this is on top.

- ✓ The removals company will want to know your completion date as soon as possible. You may not have that but give them an estimate and then update this once closer to

---

[40] Friends Pivot episode - https://www.youtube.com/watch?v=EPSpBrNyxQM

exchange.

✓ You're given a time window for your possessions to be delivered. As you are first in the chain access is likely to be from 11am, but I'd suggest getting the 2pm slot just to be safe.

✓ Check to see if you have any penalties for missing your booking window. Some removals companies charge for waiting past the allotted time.

✓ If you don't collect keys by 4pm then some removals companies may not wait and will return to their depot. You'll need to pay for delivery on the next available day which isn't always the next day.

Some removals companies offer protection for late key collection, and I think this is a good thing to have. You're not in control of when you'll collect your keys and things do happen on completion day that can cause delays.

When should you walk away from the purchase?

1 in 3 purchases fall through[41] and whilst that is sometimes because the chain breaks, the seller gets fed up, or even because the lender undervalues the property, it is sometimes you who has to walk away from the purchase. This could be for many reasons:

✓ You've lost your job and can't get a new mortgage.
✓ Your relationship breaks down with your partner.
✓ The seller doesn't provide adequate information to satisfy you of potential risks.

The loss of a job and a breakdown in the relationship are covered

---

[41] https://www.homesellingexpert.co.uk/guides/what-percentage-of-house-sales-fall-through

in *Chapter 4 - How Are You Financing the Purchase?* The issue over limited information from the seller is all too common. The risk is if you ignore the issue, buy the property and then you find out the property isn't worth what you paid for it, because the potential issue turns out to be a biggie.

There can often be a lot of pressure from the seller and the estate agent, to buy the property and ignore issues. However, it isn't they who have to live in the property or cover the cost to fix it. You'd be better off digging your heels in and setting a timeframe for the seller to provide adequate information or else you'll pull your offer and either re-offer at a lower price, or you'll walk away.

There is no shame in not proceeding with the purchase, in fact, I would strongly advise you not to buy a property you aren't 100% invested in. The cost to you could be more than if you just pulled out, waited, and found a property that was right for you, buying with a person who is right for you.

Exchange Checklist

Agree a completion date with your seller. ☐
(Speak to your estate agent and put forward a few preferred dates and see which work for the seller)

Have you read and confirmed that you are happy with the seller's Property Information Form? Double check whether: ☐

- you have a car parking space included with the property.
- the property has ever been flooded.
- the property has been affected by subsidence.

- the boundary matches what you saw during your viewing (including any garages or outbuildings).
- the property has been altered.
- you have all the warranties and guarantees for the property.

Have you read and confirmed you are happy with the seller's Fittings & Contents Form? ☐

(Inform your solicitor immediately if something is missing that the seller said they were leaving as part of the sale price)

Have you read and confirmed that you are happy with the seller's Leasehold Information From? ☐

(if leasehold – check service charges and ground rent)

Send your solicitor your signed documents: ☐

- ✓ Contract;
- ✓ Transfer document (TR1);
- ✓ Stamp Duty Land Tax Return (SDLT); and
- ✓ (If mortgage) mortgage deed.

(Do not date any of the documents and send by special delivery)

Transfer your 10% deposit ☐

(Inform your solicitor immediately if you are only paying a 5% deposit)

Contact home insurance company and activate building insurance ☐

(if freehold)

Book a completion date with your removal company

(...and check if they are available on your desired completion day)

Make sure you get your sellers onward address

(You will need this if you mistakenly receive any of their mail after the move and if they leave anything in the property after completion. This can be harder to get hold of once the transaction is finished, so get it before completion)

How To Buy a House Without Killing Anyone

CHAPTER 9

THE DAY OF COMPLETION

What happens the day before completion?

The day of completion is all about the money and the job is split between you and your solicitor:

a) Your solicitor receives the mortgage money; and

b) You send your completion monies including the balance of the money you are paying plus Stamp Duty land Tax, Land Registry fee, Solicitor fee and any other disbursements.

Some solicitors request for the mortgage advance to be sent on the day of completion, but by doing this you risk having your completion delayed, especially if it is a very busy Friday. It is safer to get the mortgage funds issued the day before. Even though you must pay mortgage interest on the extra day, the risk of a delayed completion, as we've seen in the previous chapter, can cost you more.

What happens on completion day?

As a first-time buyer you'll be at the bottom of the chain and will be the first to complete. If you and your solicitor did everything needed in the previous section, then your solicitor will release the completion money (purchase price, less any deposit already paid) to the seller's solicitor in the first payment run in the morning; normally between 8.30am and 10am.

136

Once the completion money is received by the seller's solicitor and the property is vacant, IE the seller has left the property with all their possessions, then the seller's solicitor will authorise the estate agent to release keys (for a private sale or an online agent you'll collect keys from the seller themselves).

What does a completion statement look like?
Here is an example of what your completion statement should look like[42]:

Purchase price	**£525,000**
Stamp Duty	£16,250
Land Registry	£295
Solicitor fee	£986
Property searches	£265
Lawyer Checker	£18
Misc.	£7
Less:	
Mortgage advance	£246,766
Payment made to solicitor	£160
Payment for searches	£265
10% deposit	£52,500

---

[42] https://www.samconveyancing.co.uk/news/conveyancing/compare-conveyancing-quotes#CALCULATOR

Balance to complete   £243,130

*(Send no later than the day
before completion)*

What can cause a delay?
The day of completion ought to run like clockwork because it should be just money shuffling, however, there are some things that can crop up and cause delays:

CHAPS Banking System Delay.
Solicitors send completion monies through a bank using CHAPS (Clearing House Automated Payment System). CHAPS is a bank-to-bank payment system where you can send any amount of money. CHAPS is guaranteed to be received on the same day it is transferred.

For most CHAPS transfers, the money is received within minutes, but on busy banking days the payments could take several hours to be received by the seller's solicitor.

The cut off time for sending a CHAPS is 4pm. If it is left as late as 4pm you are likely going to complete the next working day and complete with notice, interest, and penalties.

In some cases, where the seller doesn't have an onward purchase, then your solicitor may negotiate for you to move in under a licence, on the understanding that you pay for the costs of the notice to complete.

A licence means if you fail to complete the seller will find it easier to remove you from the property. Licences to move in are often used and accepted where the property is empty, the buyer's solicitor has the completion money, but there was some delay on completion, and the chance of completing the next working day are very high.

Seller can't give vacant possession.

The contract of sale will give the seller and buyer a set time to complete by, or else either side could serve a notice to complete (more on this later). The time is normally between 12pm and 2pm depending on the number of people in the chain.

You may find that even though completion monies are received by the seller's solicitor, that they delay completion until the seller is ready to move out. I've seen sellers still boxing up, right up until they hand you the keys. You can spot if this will be an issue by doing a drive-by, the night before, to see if the property looks packed up, or if there are still ornaments scattered around.

Your documents are lost in the post.

Your solicitor can't complete unless they have all your original signed documents so don't post anything by 1st or 2nd class; even Recorded Delivery isn't good enough. To avoid any delay around documents, send everything by Special Delivery, or if you are close enough to your solicitor, consider hand delivering the documents.

What happens if you complete the next working day?

Where the seller's solicitor receives completion money too late to complete, then completion will take place the next working day. The seller's solicitor will serve your solicitor with a 'Notice to Complete' which confirms:

1) you have 10 working days to complete;

2) you are liable for the notice to complete fee, for drafting the notice (normally between £120-£240 INC VAT); and

3) you are liable to pay interest on the balance due to the seller which is usually 4% above Bank of England base rate. If you owe £400,000 then a daily rate of interest is £76.71 (£400,000 * 7% (4% + BOE base of 3%) / 365)

You need to pay the interest and notice fees for completion to take place. If you fail to complete after 10 working days, then the seller can rescind the contracts and you lose your 10% deposit and your dream home.

Whilst the worst-case scenario would be for the seller to rescind the contract, you lose your deposit and pay for the legal fees of the seller, there are occasions where they'll agree to grant you an extension if they feel completion is likely to take place.

Seller has left junk in the garage, what can I do?

It is so frustrating when the seller leaves stuff in the property, whether it be junk or their precious possessions. It happens more often than it should.

It could be an honest mistake, or it could be laziness. The items, whatever their value, are the belongings of the seller, so make sure not to dispose of them for the time being.

The seller should only leave items in the property that they stated were included within the purchase price in their TA10 Fittings and Contents Form. It says in that form *"The aim of this form is to make clear to the buyer which items are included in the sale. It must be completed accurately by the seller as the form may become part of the contract between the buyer and seller"*.

The legal position is *"Unless stated otherwise, the seller will be responsible for ensuring that all rubbish is removed from the property (including from the loft, garden, outbuildings, garages and shed), and that the property is left in a reasonably clean and tidy condition"*.

If there is stuff left by the seller you should:

1. **Inform your solicitor.** Your solicitor will contact the seller's

solicitor and request the seller come back and collect their stuff. You should keep their stuff safe and secure. If it is mess which you want the seller to tidy, then leave it as is for now. Take pictures and a video as evidence.

2. **Start legal proceedings for your loss.** If the seller fails to return, then you can start legal proceedings for the losses incurred. You can make a Money Claim online (up to £10,000[43]), but you'll need the address of the seller so make sure you get the seller's onward address prior to completion.

Whilst you can make a claim, sometimes it is easier to get rid of the items yourself and make your new home yours.

A tip for spotting whether this is going to be an issue, is to do a viewing a few days before completion to see how the seller is getting on with boxing up their stuff.

Completion Checklist

Ask your solicitor to draw down your mortgage funds the **day before** completion.	☐
Transfer your balance to complete the day before completion. (Including stamp duty, land registry and solicitor fees)	☐
If not informed beforehand, chase your solicitor no earlier than 11am to confirm if completion has taken place.	☐

---

[43] https://www.gov.uk/make-court-claim-for-money

Contact home insurance company and activate contents insurance. ☐

For freeholds building insurance is taken out on exchange.

Collect your keys to the property. ☐

Including front door, back door, shed, gates, side doors garage and windows; you need all the keys to the whole of the property. This also means getting access codes to the alarm.

Inform removal company that you have completed and provide access to move in. ☐

Check the property is empty of all the seller's property. ☐

Don't forget the garage, shed and loft – call you solicitor immediately if there are any items left.

Check the items the seller agreed to leave you in the Fittings & Contents forms have been left in the property. ☐

Call your solicitor immediately if any items are missing. If there are the read Chapter 9 - Seller has left junk in the garage, what can I do?

Take note of the meter readings. ☐

Not sure where the meters are? Check outside of the property or in the downstairs cupboard.

Gas meter number:	
Gas reading:	
Electric meter number:	
Electric reading:	
Water meter number:	
Water reading:	

Call the utility providers to give them the meter readings. ☐

Turn on/off the heating. Set up the heating so the property is heated to your liking. ☐

The seller rarely has it set the way you'll like it so update the heating to make the property as comfortable as you like it to be.

Request your solicitor apply a Form LL Restriction. ☐

This is an Anti-Fraud Restriction that stops criminals from impersonating you and stealing your home. We cover this more in *Chapter 10 - How can I protect my property from fraud?*

Order fresh food. ☐

An online order delivered the day after completion will save you one job whilst you're up to your eyes in boxes.

I'd also suggest ordering your favourite takeaway for completion day night. Trying to find pots and pans (and even the food) is too much hassle so why not enjoy a treat and take in the feeling of being in your new home.

CHAPTER 10

YOU'RE NO LONGER A FIRST-TIME BUYER, NOW WHAT?

Day 1 in your own home.

First, work out where you packed the kettle because day 1 is surreal. You've battled long and hard to achieve this goal and now you are no longer a first-time buyer. Your foot is firmly on the ladder.

There are a few jobs you mustn't forget amidst unpacking (in order of priority – tick off as you go):

Broadband. This is the first job because it takes 2 weeks for Openreach to connect your broadband/telephone line.

You can't pay for it to be done quicker, so if you need broadband then you need to order this on the day of completion (or if you are willing to take the risk, in case completion is delayed, on the day of exchange) to reduce the time without internet.

Update bank accounts, credit cards and store cards.

As we saw earlier, you need to have all your records updated to your new address to maintain a strong credit score, it also reduces the risk of fraud if the new tenants in your old property open your mail. Including stamp duty, land registry and solicitor fees.

Royal Mail Redirection.

You can pay to get your mail directed from your old address to your new one. Each time you get a letter through you can then contact the company and update your new home address.

Update Utility Providers.
Call your utility providers and provide your meter readings. If you are slow in doing this, you don't need to worry, because utility providers will continue to supply your property. You will also need to call the Local Authority to cancel any Council Tax you were paying for at your rented property (you might even get a little rebate!) and register yourselves at your new home.

Land Registry Property Alerts.
Sign up to the Land Registry's free title register alert service44 that informs you if there are any changes to your property's title. You can now have up to 4 addresses on the title, one of which can be abroad, and one can be an email. This is important, and the onus is on you to keep the register updated with your current address.

Say hi to the neighbours.
In sitcoms you see the new neighbours turn up with cake to say "Hi", which is a nice idea, but not practical when you can't even find where you packed the kettle. You'll be living next door to your neighbours for a good few years so strike up an early relationship, maybe after you've settled in.

What does my solicitor do after completion?
Who files/pays my Stamp Duty Land Tax?
After completion your solicitor will file your stamp duty land tax return to HMRC and they will pay any tax due, within 14 days. You need to file a tax return even if there is no tax to pay.

How long does it take to update the Land Registry?
Since Covid, the Land Registry has been struggling to register the volume of property updates that have taken place and it is taking between 6 to 24 months to update the title ownership. If you need to sell, remortgage, or update the title for any reason and your property hasn't been registered to your name yet then you can inform the Land Registry and they will expedite your purchase

---

44 https://www.gov.uk/protect-land-property-from-fraud

registration.

The main thing is that even though it isn't updated yet, it doesn't really matter. You have your keys, you've moved in, so just leave the admin to the solicitor, and enjoy your new home knowing you managed to buy a house without killing anyone.

Neighbours, everybody needs good neighbours!

"With a little understanding..." Although neighbours the TV series has ended, the need to strike up good relationships with your neighbours hasn't. Here's a few reasons why:

- ✓ House watching when you're on holiday so they can help if there is an issue or even call you if something is wrong.
- ✓ They can look after your deliveries (saves them sitting outside your front door).
- ✓ You can share the school run if your kids are the same age.
- ✓ They can help in an emergency.
- ✓ If you share a drain and it gets blocked you can share the cost to fix.
- ✓ They've live in the area longer than you so will know good local plumbers, electricians and other local tradesman.
- ✓ Share power tools and garden equipment.
- ✓ You might even *"...become good friends!"*

If you think your home is a castle separate to everyone else, then you'll miss out on the community spirit that can be achieved through helping your neighbour. If there is an issue, such as a boundary dispute or a late-night house party, you're more likely to resolve it with a neighbour you a close to, than one you are arguing with.

What happens next?

How can I protect my property from fraud?

A major risk when owning your property is the potential for someone to impersonate you and sell your property without you knowing. Sounds mad, but this happens all too frequently. Here are some real-life examples:

1. Fraudsters sold Mr Hall's Luton property without his knowledge, whilst he was away in Wales. The house had been emptied and works had begun before he found out what had happened and the new owner had no idea the property had been sold fraudulently[45].
2. Mr Penfound lost his buy to let property in Southampton, after fraudsters sold it. The Land Registry are allowing the innocent new owners to keep it, as they were already living in the premises when he was alerted to the problem by the council, who contacted him regarding an unpaid council tax bill[46].

To protect against this, you can apply a Form LL restriction on your title at the Land Registry. The restriction protects your house from being registered to a new owner, if criminals use your identity to sell your property, as they would be unable to do so without getting a solicitor to verify that they were you.

The restriction states: "No disposition of the registered estate by the proprietor of the registered estate is to be registered without a certificate signed by a conveyancer that the conveyancer is satisfied that the person who executed the document submitted for registration as disponer is the same person as the proprietor". In simpler terms this means you can't sell/transfer (dispense) the property without you getting a certificate from a solicitor who verifies you are the person named on the title.

This means that any time you want to do something to the title, like register a loan, add your partner to the deed, or sell the house. You'll have to verify your identity with a solicitor, in a face-to-face meeting, often on video call, to verify you and your ID and to check they are the same as the names on the legal title. The solicitor will provide a certificate, and this will then be passed on to the Land Registry through the solicitor acting for you on the sale/remortgage/transfer of equity.

---

[45] https://www.independent.co.uk/news/uk/home-news/house-sold-property-fraud-luton-b1949238.html
[46] https://www.dailyecho.co.uk/news/23093949.hampshire-man-left-without-words-finding-house-sold-without-knowing/

The downside is that although it only costs £40 to apply the restriction[47], each and every time you want to remortgage, transfer equity or sell, you need to pay a solicitor to provide this certificate. The cost ranges from £150 to £200[48]. Whilst this is an expense, it does mean that unless a criminal has facial reconstruction to look like you and can forge your signature perfectly, there is no way the property can be sold without you knowing.

What happens if I can't afford to repay my mortgage?

In 2022 we saw Bank of England base rate increases up to 3% and it is set to go up to 5% in 2023. If you only got a fixed rate mortgage for 2 years, then by the time your mortgage fixed term expired, the doubling interest rate could mean that you'll struggle to pay the mortgage repayments at the new interest rate.

With an increase in mortgage interest added onto the financial burden of increased utility costs, fixing that broken boiler, changing the electrics, buying new white goods, paying to unblock the drains because your neighbours have just had a kid and they are flushing their wet wipes down the toilet; these costs could mount up and before you know it you could be firmly in your overdraft, using pay day loans and damaging your credit history.

Before this happens, if you anticipate that you are going to struggle to pay, you need to:

1) **Contact your mortgage lender**. Your mortgage lender may offer guidance on what you can do, such as mortgage holidays or different payment terms. These options can affect your credit score.

---

[47] https://www.gov.uk/government/publications/enter-a-restriction-registration-rx1
[48] https://www.parachutelaw.co.uk/form-ll-land-registry-restriction

2) **Cut back expenses**. Gym memberships, betting, Netflix, Sky, holidays, cinema, pub nights, restaurants, and take-aways – all of these can be stopped and can save you £100s a month. You should also put together a budget and stick to it for food and alcohol. Plus, don't go shopping without your "shopping list" and only buy what is on your list.

3) **Part-time job**. Whether working behind a bar or cleaning, these jobs can be done outside of the 9-5 day and are good ways to earn more money and make the cost of living more affordable. If cash in hand, don't forget to put money away for the tax payable on this income and declare it in your end of year tax return.

4) **Sell and rent**. It sounds drastic but so is being repossessed and whilst lenders will work with homeowners to find solutions, the goodwill only lasts so long. Missing mortgage repayments seriously damages your credit score, so even though you may find a solution with your lender, if you're struggling you may find it less stressful to sell and move back into rented accommodation.

5) **Get help from a family member**. Whilst it may not be an option for everyone, you could speak to your family and see if they'd help you with your mortgage repayments. If they do this then be clear on whether the money they pay is a loan, a gift, or if they are expecting a beneficial interest in the property (as discussed in the Deed of Trust section).

Your lender should understand if your household income has dropped because of unexpected events such as:

• a job loss in the family, for example if you were made redundant,
• an illness or accident, or
• a death.

Many lenders have specialist support teams who can explain what options they have.

What can your lender do to help?

Mortgage lenders have a duty to treat you fairly and consider your request to change the way you pay your mortgage. Depending on your circumstances, your lender might offer you the option to:

- change when you pay - you might be able to take a break from paying your mortgage,

- repay what you owe at a later date - you could arrange to have what you owe added to the capital outstanding on the mortgage. This is called 'capitalising the arrears',

- reduce the amount you pay for a short period of time - you might be able to pay less towards your mortgage for the next few months,

- repay your mortgage over a longer period - this is called extending the mortgage term,

- reduce your monthly interest payments - you might be able to negotiate a lower interest rate if you have equity in your property,

- change to interest-only payments - this is where you only pay off the interest on what you borrow each month,

- switch to a cheaper mortgage - you might be able to reduce your payments by changing to a fixed-rate mortgage.

What can you do if you go into negative equity?

Being in negative equity can be very scary because you currently own a property that if you sold it, it wouldn't pay off the mortgage; let along the estate agent fees and legal fees. This can happen for a number of reasons:

1) A development in the local area such as HS2
2) A breach of a restrictive covenant, Easement/Right on the property
3) A housing market crash, such as seen in 2007

Whilst it is scary, the main thing is that if you can afford to repay your mortgage, then negative equity isn't an issue. You can pay off more and more of the mortgage debt until the equity is more than the mortgage debt. The issue arises when you can't afford your mortgage repayments and you can't sell because you can't afford to repay the mortgage. In these cases, you need to speak to your mortgage lender as soon as possible and see what help they can provide you.

I hope you found the book useful, and it is now full of highlights and post-it tabs so you can go back over them again. If you know of anyone struggling with buying their house, then please share the book. My goal is to help as many people as I can with this book...and stop them killing anyone!

JARGON BUSTING GLOSSARY

Term	Meaning
Beneficial Owner	The name/s of the people who have a beneficial interest in the property. It is often held 50:50 between the legal owners but it can be any percentage split. You can also have a non-legal owner who has a beneficial interest and could get paid money on the sale of the property. I cover this more in: Be careful who moves into your property!
Chattels	These are items that are being charged in addition to the purchase price that will be part of the sale. For example, buying the seller's sofa and TV costing £1,000 on top of the agreed offer price for the property.
Certificate of Title	The approved certificate of title is the document the conveyancing solicitor gives to the lender to confirm certain statements about the property.

The certificate confirms to the lender:

- ✓ there are no legal problems with the property – it has a "good and marketable title" - so the lender can safely lend against it;
- ✓ who will own the property once the sale is completed; and

✓ the completion date when the funds are needed.

Completion	This is the day your solicitor pays the seller's solicitor the balance of the purchase price for the property, and you collect your keys – and unpack lots of boxes.
Conveyancing	The process of moving the legal ownership of property or land from one person to another.
Constructive Trust	A constructive trust arises where the intention of the parties is to share the beneficial interest of property/land (also known as equitable interest, meaning the share of any gain or loss on sale/transfer) between each other.
Contract of Sale	This is drafted by the seller's solicitor based on the details in the sales memo. It includes the agreed price, chattels, names and addresses of the seller and buyer and the address of the property and title number/s.
Deed of Trust	A legal document drafted to set out the intentions for the property and to state the beneficial interest split between tenants in common. For example, I own 60% and you own 40% and you agree how to sell the property in the future.
Deed of Variation	A standard document used to vary the terms of a lease (leasehold agreement), as agreed by the relevant freeholder and leaseholder/s and

sometimes other parties, such as lenders.

Deposit
You pay a deposit on exchange of contracts which is normally 10% of the purchase price. This is held by the seller's solicitor unless agreed otherwise.

Draft Contracts
This is the packet of documents provided by the seller to the buyer's solicitor and includes:

- ✓ Contract of sale
- ✓ Property Information Forms - TA6, TA10 and TA7 (if applicable)
- ✓ Office copy
- ✓ Title Plan
- ✓ Original Transfer
- ✓ EPC
- ✓ Warranties and guaranties for the property
- ✓ (If leasehold) Leasehold Management Pack

Easements and Rights
Having an easement on your property means that another, usually adjoining or nearby property owner or utility company has a right to come onto or pass over your property, for a particular purpose. They could have a right to come on to your property on foot, or with vehicles, at restricted times or at any time, or they may have a right to use or connect into the services that run under your land, or a right over a footpath to access a bin store etc.

For example, a burden or a benefit relating to

rights of light, rights of way, rights of support, easements/services.

Enquiries

Legal enquiries are the questions the buyer's solicitor raises for the seller's solicitor to reply to, following a review of all the legal documents. They often relate to clarification or request for further information.

Energy Performance Certificate (EPC)

An EPC gives a property an energy efficiency rating from A (most efficient) to G (least efficient) and is valid for 10 years. A seller can't market their property without a an in-date EPC.

Exchange of Contracts

This is the day you become legally bound to buy the property and pay a deposit to the seller's solicitor.

Freehold

The property you are buying is a house and you own the land underneath it. You sometimes have freeholds where you have a liability to pay a rent charge to maintain the grounds in the local community.

Freeholder

The owner of a freehold when you are buying a leasehold. They may have a managing agent to manage the freehold.

HMRC

HM Revenue and Customs receive your Stamp Duty Land Tax and payment for any tax within 14 days after completion.

Joint Tenants

As joint tenants (sometimes called 'beneficial

joint tenants'):

- you have equal rights to the whole property.
- the property automatically goes to the other owners if you die.
- you cannot pass on your ownership of the property in your will.

Land Registry Formed in 1861 the HM Land Registry registers the ownership of property.

Leasehold The property you are buying has a lease which means the freehold is owned by someone else. The lease has a set number of years and sets out what you can do in the property, what the freeholder is obligated to do and ground rent (if applicable).

Leasehold Management Pack This is purchased by the seller, normally through their solicitor, from their Freeholder/Managing Agent. It contains statements for ground rent, service charges, planned major works to the freehold/communal areas, and financial accounts for the last 3 years.

Legal Owner The name/s registered at the Land Registry.

Legal Title (title deeds) This is what you are buying. It is the legal title to live in the property that is what you are buying. For a freehold there is one title. For a leasehold there is a separate leasehold title and a freehold title, but you are buying the leasehold title. There are occasions where you have another title as part of the purchase such as a garage or a parcel of land with your garden.

Managing Agent
Employed by the freeholder to manage the freehold on behalf of them.

Memorandum of Sale (sales memo)
A memorandum of sale is created by the selling estate agent and records the amount of money being paid for a property and any conditions agreed such as time frames or chattels. It includes the names and addresses of both the property seller and buyer, and the names of the solicitors dealing with both parties.

Negative Equity
Negative equity is when your property becomes worth less than the remaining value of your mortgage. To be in negative equity, the value of your house must fall below the amount you still owe on your mortgage. For example, if your property is currently worth £200,000 but the mortgage debt is £210,000, then you are currently £10,000 in negative equity.

Official Copy of the Register (Office Copy)
Official register means the official record furnished to election officials by the election officer that contains the information required by Section 20A-5-401. You can download it for £3 from the Land Registry if the property is

registered[49].

Original Transfer	The transfer document between the original landowner (transferor) to the original buyer (transferee). It'll contain the details of the sale and easements, rights, and restrictive covenants.
Replies to Requisitions	This refers to the seller's solicitor's response to the questions you solicitor asked in Form TA13. These are essential for the purchase to complete and impose undertakings on the seller's solicitor.
Report on Title	Contains the findings of the solicitor's investigation on the title including any charges, easements or parties possessing an interest or potential interest, as well as any rights from which the land benefits.
Restrictive Covenants	A restrictive covenant is a contract between 2 (or more) landowners, where one (or more) promise the other landowner(s) not to carry out certain acts on their own land. They are usually created when one party sells part of their land and wishes to restrict what the buyer can do with the land following the sale. Sometimes, they can affect the sellers land as well. The obligation to comply with the

---

[49] https://www.gov.uk/search-property-information-land-registry

restrictive covenant remains no matter how often the land changes hands or how old they are.

For example, you may have a restrictive covenant stopping you from running a business from your property.

Restrictions   A restriction is an entry on the Title of the property, that prevents you from selling, transferring, or gifting the property or registering a new mortgage (all these terms collectively called a "disposition") the property, or that transaction being registered at HM Land Registry unless and until the conditions contained in the Restriction are met.

For example, a Form LL restriction requires you to get your ID certified and a certificate issued so you can make a disposition on the title.

Resulting Trust   A resulting trust is formed by the contribution towards the purchase price of the property, or directly towards renovations/repairs or towards the mortgage repayments (as agreed prior to purchase).

Share of Freehold   The property you are buying is a leasehold, but you are also going to own a share of the freehold. This means you along with the other share of freeholders need to deliver on the freeholders' obligations in the lease.

Standard Variable Rate	A standard variable rate, or SVR, is the interest rate that will be charged once an initial deal period on a fixed or tracker rate mortgage comes to an end. With an SVR mortgage, your mortgage payments could change each month, going up or down depending on the rate. While lenders tend to adjust their SVR along the lines of the BoE base rate, they can set their SVR rate however they like, so beware that a reduction in the base rate wont necessarily reduce your SVR, just as your bank may up their SVR by a greater increase than the base rate.
TA6 Property Information Form	This form is for the seller to give the prospective buyer detailed information about the property such as works they've done or issues that they encountered during their ownership.
TA7 Leasehold Information Form	This form is for the seller to give the prospective buyer detailed information about the freeholder, managing agent and their leasehold obligations such as service charge and ground rent.
TA10 Fittings and Contents Form	This form is for the seller to give the prospective buyer detailed information about what items are being left as part of the purchase price in the contract, what they are taking and what they are prepared to sell.
Tenants In	When you buy a property with someone else

Common   you can either buy it as tenants in common or joint tenants. As tenants in common:

- you can own different shares of the property.
- the property does not automatically go to the other owners if you die.
- you can pass on your share of the property in your will.

Title Number   The number applied to the title you are buying at the Land Registry. Your property address is what you use, but the Land Registry use a title number (like an index number).

Title Plan   A drawing of the boundary of the property you are buying.

Undertakings   A firm professional agreement from a solicitor, to carry out some action faithfully and within required time frames. It is a promise that cannot be broken.

Vacant Possession   This means that the property is empty of people and property on your completion day, other than the items listed in your TA10 Fittings and Contents Form.

ABOUT THE AUTHOR

Andrew has been working in the conveyancing sector since 2000 and co-founded SAM Conveyancing in 2014, to provide buyers with straight talking support that isn't influenced by the seller or their estate agent.

His journey toward writing this book began as a legal cashier in a Guildford based law firm. His career has provided a real understanding of the process from the numbers to the strategy, to the real-life experiences of over 50,000 movers.

Andrew identified and filled a niche in the industry, a gap between the risk averse and phone avoidant solicitor and the communication-hungry client.

He has provided guidance and opinion to the majority of the mainstream news media and has appeared on the BBC, ITV and London Live; as well as uncovering exclusions within the Help to Buy Scheme which adversely affected over 500,000[50] first time buyers.

If you'd like to get in touch, drop him a line at *help@samconveyancing.co.uk*

---

[50] https://www.telegraph.co.uk/news/2016/08/19/help-to-buy-isa-scandal-500000-first-time-buyers-told-scheme-can/

Printed in Great Britain
by Amazon

19749042R00103